PRAYEROBICS

Getting Started and Staying Going

PRAYEROBICS

CECIL
MURPHEY

WORD BOOKS
PUBLISHER
4800 WEST WACO DRIVE
WACO, TEXAS
76703

PRAYEROBICS

ISBN   0-8499-0146-4
Library of Congress Catalog Card No: 79-63934
Printed in the United States of America

To Michael

Contents

Introduction

As I STEPPED out of the shower and began drying off, I caught a glimpse of myself in the mirror. For a long minute I stared at that figure.

While my head knew quite well that my body had experienced forty years of life, my eyes suddenly made me aware that I looked like all of my forty years. That inward image my mind carried around of a slim, trim, wrinkleless, twenty-five-year-old crumbled before me. The hairline had receded. That youthful skin showed deep wrinkles I had never noticed before. The flat stomach now puffed out as though swollen by malnutrition.

Nobody needed to tell me what had happened to my body in the past fifteen years. No intelligent person could ignore those changes either. I had become a pudgy, wrinkled, middle-aged man. My blood pressure, according to a physical the previous week, had soared to a borderline danger point. Simply running across the church parking lot winded me.

"You'll never see twenty-five again," I said aloud, and sighed. It wasn't that I wanted to *be* twenty-five; I only wanted to *look* twenty-five. At least I didn't want to remain what I saw in the mirror.

Before sunset I had developed a plan for daily exercise. Sit-ups, push-ups, leg raises, rope jumping—every morning. For three weeks I was faithful. By the fourth week, not only had I given up, but the bathroom scales demeaned me further by insisting I had gained two pounds.

For the next year the war raged. One week I'd lose two pounds, and then gain one back the following week. Or I'd gain three and lose only two. One week's weight loss seemed always to trigger an easing up the next.

Finally—on February 23, 1975 at 8:15 P.M.—that all changed.

The time to face reality had come. I talked to myself (I really did—and out loud, too!). "Cec, you're getting nowhere this way. You need to shape up, and you're going to do it."

I started a fitness program that I've continued, with modifications, to the present day. My body shrank twenty-five pounds, which have remained off. You can count two extra notches in all my belts, and my neck size now measures one full size smaller. My blood pressure hovers in the beautifully low-normal range. Nothing happened to decrease wrinkles, but now that I'm slimmer I don't mind. I can run five miles and not gasp for breath. Most of all, I feel better than I have in years.

From the time I started on my fitness program, I've done a lot of reading and asked many questions. I've learned about nutrition and physical fitness. And I've stayed on my program with only minor setbacks. I continue to watch what I eat and to maintain a physical regimen. My biggest reward came recently when I was going through some old papers and records. My military discharge fell out. As I looked at it I realized that I now weighed two pounds *less* than I had twenty years ago!

As I look back, I realize that several factors entered into my whole shape-up program. But I started by becoming dissatisfied with the old me. I also saw my need to be better than I was. By accepting where I was, and by projecting in my mind where I wanted to be, I moved forward.

That's also the story of this book. I call it *Prayerobics,* because it presents some guidelines I have learned over the years for improving spiritual fitness. It suggests some ways to start and maintain a more effective prayer life. If you are dissatisfied with your spiritual self-image and want to grow in your relationship to Jesus Christ, perhaps some of my *Prayerobics* secrets can help you.

Yes, I said *secrets.* The following incident may help you understand what I mean:

After giving me a careful look, my friend Julie asked, "Want to know a secret?"

"Sure," I answered, glad to hear a secret, even from a nine-year-old.

"Well," she said, lowering her voice slightly, "zebras have *brown* stripes and not black."

"But Julie," I blurted out, "that's not a secret. Zebras have been around a long time and I knew ..."

"Well, *I* didn't know until yesterday. And if I didn't know, then it was still a secret, wasn't it?"

As I think about Julie's concept of a secret, it occurs to me that effective praying fits into the same category. I haven't written anything in this book that's been hidden from the world or is now revealed by the Holy Spirit for the first time in history. But what I've written were secrets to me until I understood them. And I believe they have helped me achieve a more effective prayer life, a more dynamic witness for Christ.

I'm not asking you to read a chapter a day or to begin a thirty-day program. But I am offering you simple, practical, easy-to-do helps with reflective questions at the end of each chapter. You can do this as an individual or in a group study. I hope the ideas I have to share will help you get into spiritual shape and keep going for the rest of your life!

1
The Phrase I Hate to Hear

PERHAPS IT'S THAT I've heard it too often. Or because I suspect it's only a smokescreen people use to excuse themselves. More truthfully, I don't like it because I once used it myself! The phrase goes like this: "I know I don't pray as much as I ought, but..."

Whenever someone starts that sentence, I can feel myself tightening up, almost ready to hear a harangue of self-justification. The people who start their sentences with the phrase I hate to hear usually add, "but I'm so busy with my job ... my family ... my church activities ... my fast-paced life ... my wedding plans ... my emotional problems ... my homework ... my broken home ... my troubled marriage ... my insomnia ..." The list seems endless. There's always an excuse.

And it's not only about prayer. For instance, a few weeks ago in a seminar, I spoke for an hour on how to have a more meaningful private Bible study. Sure enough, one man raised his hand. "Mr. Murphey, I don't read my Bible as much as I ought to, but ..." Or when I mention giving money to the Lord's work, I can predict that before the evening ends at least one person will say, "We don't give as much money to God as we ought, but ..."

People offer my hated phrase because they're so guilt-laden that any talk of commitment would trigger this reaction. Not that some guilt isn't helpful; true guilt can lead to inner conviction and a change of direction. But somehow people have developed so much guilt over their spiritual paucity that, no matter how long they actually pray, there's always the nagging sense that they ought to be praying longer. Or more frequently. Certainly more fervently.

Where does this idea come from that we have to live and breathe prayer every moment of our waking day? Perhaps we preacher-types have inculcated the idea that true Christians spend fifteen hours a day on our knees in communion with God. What a guilt trip to read some of the devotional literature of the early Puritan period, or to study the great Protestant reformers. It was said of Martin Luther that he allowed no day to pass without giving God at least three of his best hours in prayer. John Calvin supposedly spent as much time on his knees. Richard Baxter wrote not only of length of time in prayer, but of the importance of fervency as well.

These men were great Christians, and I admire them greatly. But they lived in a different culture, and in a slower-paced world. Not to recognize that difference is absurd.

I recall reading the biography of "Praying John Hyde," the missionary who, at the turn of this century, was so greatly used by God. I wanted to imitate him. He had begun with an hour a day in prayer and worked up to two hours daily, then three. Each year he prayed more and more.

What a challenge to me! If Hyde could do it, why couldn't I?

In order to follow his example, I had to get up at 4:00 A.M. and pray. I made it the first three mornings, and even thought about getting up at 3:30 A.M. the following week. About the fifth day, however, I dozed during my prayer. By the end of the week I realized that, as much as I admired Praying Hyde, I couldn't imitate him.

I felt guilty for a long time. After all, I reasoned, he was only a man like myself, wasn't he? But one day Shirley said, "Honey, you're not Praying Hyde, and God doesn't expect you to live like him. You don't have his kind of temperament—you're too much of the activist type. And God expects you to be yourself."

Praying John Hyde may have felt the need for six hours of daily prayer. I've never felt that kind of need. And I don't think I could live that style of life. Shirley knows me well; I'm an active, on-the-run type of person. Perhaps an hour a day, but three? Even four? *Every* day? Definitely not for me!

I think there's another reason people use my disliked phrase, and this is a corollary of the guilt issue. I wonder if people aren't unconsciously saying, "Tell me I'm still okay, even though I don't live up to my highest ideals."

A few months ago a young man sat in my office. For at least fifteen minutes he poured out his story; in his young years he had seen more of the seamy side of life than any person ought to experience in a full lifetime.

"I know I'm not as good as I ought to be, but . . ." Then he started telling me of his poor environment, indifferent parents, his other problems. He was giving about the sixth reason when I finally interrupted him.

"Rob, it doesn't matter. You don't have to justify the things you did. You did a lot of things you're ashamed of. Right?"

"Yeah, yeah, I guess that's what I mean to say."

Our session continued. I wanted to help Rob in his striving to live a better life. I also felt that what he needed was to be convinced that I understood his failures, that I liked him anyway.

I've often wondered when people say, "I know I should pray more, *but* . . ." if those words don't unconsciously say the same thing Rob was saying: "Please understand me." Or even "Tell me it's okay that I don't pray more than I do." And I want to interrupt them as I did Rob and tell them, "You don't have to justify your prayer life to me. Just be honest with yourself and we can work from there."

Delores comes to mind. A homemaker with two children in grammar school, she sends her husband off to work and her children to the school bus by 8:15 every morning. It takes her less than an hour to wash dishes, make beds, and straighten up the house. Then what? She faithfully follows six different soap operas each day. She also reads one novel a week. But I recall that once, in an informal group, Delores commented, "I know I ought to pray more, but I just can't find the time."

I'm not objecting to Delores's watching television soap operas.

After all, that's her privilege as she regulates her own life. What troubles me is the mental dishonesty involved. Had she said, "Sometimes I feel guilty about not praying more, but prayer really isn't that important to me," then I could nod in understanding. That would have sounded more like an honest statement.

We all establish priorities in our lives. Delores gives TV time a high rating. Does she feel guilty over that? Probably. Another person gives priority to a job, another to social activities.

A prominent husband and wife in our congregation came to me one morning. Circles under her eyes and a dull look about his face immediately notified me that trouble had descended upon their lives. Their teenaged son, the closest person to their hearts, had gotten into trouble. The police had arrested him. While the offense was minor, the incident was major to them. They sensed their failure as parents and agonized over the rebellious action of their son.

"I know I ought to spend more time at home with him," the father said to me, "and I try, but I can't quit work."

"You spend exactly as much time with him as you really want to," I said. And somehow I knew that statement was right. The father had actually given his son a slot in the priority list—but a position near the bottom. The father and son did meet at breakfast every morning—but usually not any other time *but* breakfast. The father was too involved in other things.

It seems to me that one of the first elements about a growing relationship with God is the ability to be honest with ourselves. When I face up to and admit my desires—or my lack of desire—then I'm in the right starting place. One of my college professors, a church member and a lay leader, once said to a group of us, "Prayer has never been a very significant force in my life." I wish that his devotional life had been more significant, but at least he didn't try to fool himself or us.

I recall hearing a student friend during my early days in college speak up in a Sunday school class. It was a class in which a lot of spiritual one-upmanship went on, in which every person who spoke had a little better testimony than the previous one. Stories of great experiences or implications of great spiritual depth permeated the remarks. Finally Frank, normally a quiet person, spoke up.

"I don't know much about Jesus Christ, and I haven't had much experience. I can say only one thing: I am hungry to know more. And I thank God that he gave me that hunger." The remark stopped the flow of conversation, and no one responded for a moment. Finally one young lady, who had been rather vocal about her spiritual growth, spoke up, "That's what I really need—more of a hunger for God."

We have as much of God as we want at any one time. If we're hungry, we'll seek after God. If we're satisfied, we'll not ask. It's that simple. I'll read the Bible only if I'm convinced that it will enable me to mature spiritually, and only if I really want to mature. I only pray when I sense my need.

A few weeks ago, Marilyn said, "I don't go to church as often as I ought, *but . . .*"

"Are you sure?" I asked her.

A confused look painted her face for a moment. "Hmm," she finally said, "That's wrong, isn't it? I go as often as I really want to go. I guess my trouble is that I've not made the effort." She paused for a few more seconds, and then said, "I also think that I'm not quite sure I want to make a full commitment of myself to Jesus Christ. I've been wrestling with this for several weeks."

We talked quite awhile. Before she left, she said, "Thanks for making me face those things about myself. You know, I really was prepared to offer you a long list of reasons for not being faithful at church. But they all seem insignificant now."

I hate to hear the phrase, "I know I ought to, *but . . .*" However, I imagine people will be using it for a long time. I hope we can help them drop that excuse-laden statement. I hope we can help them accept their present relationship with themselves and with Jesus Christ.

Questions for Thought
and Discussion

1. How do you react when people excuse or justify their lack of prayerfulness? Do you frequently use "the phrase I hate to hear"?
2. One of my college professors honestly admitted prayer played no large part in his life. Would you respect his statement more than that of Delores? Why?
3. Do you pray as much as you feel you *ought*? On a piece of paper write down all the excuses you can think of for not praying more. How many of them can you see as really valid reasons for not praying?
4. How can you know when you pray "enough"? What kind of guidelines can you offer others in answering this question?
5. Do you think the amount of time spent in prayer is especially important? Are some people who pray little as spiritual as those who pray more? Does maturing in your faith mean you'll spend greater amounts of time with God? The same? Perhaps less?
6. Who is the most *godly* person you know—either personally or by reading or hearing about? Why did you select that individual? What most about his or her life attracted you?
7. Do you feel guilty for not praying more than you do? How can we help people who use the phrase I hate to hear?
8. Why do most people use that phrase? Is it a cover-up? Would you be comfortable challenging a person who makes that statement?
9. On a piece of paper, write down the activities you could drop if you really wanted to spend more time with God. How many additional hours could you find if you really wanted to?
10. On that same piece of paper, write down the activities you

engage in (outside of your employment) each week. Beside each activity, jot down the hours you spend. How many hours for TV? Recreation? Sports? If you based your priorities strictly on the amount of time you spend, what item would have the number one spot?

11. (This question is for private meditation.) Ask yourself, How much time do I spend praying each day? Do I honestly feel that I *ought* to spend more time? How much of a difference is there between "am" and "ought"? If there's a difference, do you intend to do anything about it?

2

Hoofing It

"I DO MOST OF MY PRAYING on the hoof," the wife of a famous evangelist said. "With my busy schedule . . ."

"Praying on the hoof?" queried the interviewer.

"That means I do most of my praying while washing dishes, brushing my teeth, or even driving the car. Things like that."

"But don't you set aside regular time each day for prayer?"

She paused for a moment before answering, "I try to. But I don't always succeed every day in getting alone. And I think God hears me when I'm weeding my flowers just as much as when I'm on my knees."

One of my close friends in college had a similar attitude. I had come to him about my own problems with a set devotional time. I got out of bed in the morning, but couldn't seem to stay awake while reading my Bible or praying. I recognized Rocky as a deeply committed Christian.

"I don't set aside a special time," he said, "but I spend much time in prayer. For me, prayer is an attitude in my life. I'm constantly interceding for people. I walk about in fellowship with God almost every waking moment."

Because I knew Rocky well, and because I had great respect for the wife of the famous evangelist, I accepted their words, although some people might have used those same phrases as pious cover-ups for not praying on any regular basis. I understood them because they seemed to be saying what Brother Lawrence had said three centuries earlier.

Brother Lawrence, a lay worker in a monastery, wrote a classic of devotional literature, *The Practice of the Presence of God.* His single aim was to be always in conscious, personal union with God. He struggled to be aware of the Lord's presence every waking moment. "A kitchen and an altar were as one to him; and to pick up straw from the ground was as grand a service as to preach to multitudes." *

Brother Lawrence himself said, "The time of business does not with me differ from the time of prayer; and in the noise and clutter of my kitchen, while several persons are at the same time calling for different things, I possess God in as great tranquility as if I were upon my knees at the blessed sacrament."

This unusual man believed that a person could get into the habit ("practice") of being aware of the presence of God in every waking moment. He felt that at any time, in the middle of any duty, under any circumstances, the soul that wants to know God can "practice the presence."

Some years ago I read another classic, Frank Laubach's *Letters by a Modern Mystic.* Laubach yearned for what he called a "moment-by-moment" contact with Jesus Christ. He also struggled for that unbroken relationship while about his normal duties.

For years I've admired these spiritual giants. Imagine, being constantly aware of Christ's presence. Nothing distracting or pulling away. A relationship so close that all of life is lived on hallowed ground. A sense of being always in the divine sanctuary.

I've tried it, too. I've tried praying "on the hoof." Meaningful experiences have come out of it. An experience with Wes comes to mind. I had tried to like him, but found it difficult. Whenever we talked, he constantly needled me about my faith in Christ. Not outright sneering, which would have been easy enough to respond to. More subtle, he smiled and laughed at the faith—always in a way that wasn't quite offensive.

---

* Brother Lawrence, *The Practice of the Presence of God, being Conversations and Letters of Nicholas Herman of Lorrane, Brother Lawrence* (New York: Fleming H. Revell, 1895), p. 8.

One day we sat next to each other at a luncheon. I knew he'd
be at me for the next hour or longer. Only days before, I had
reread portions of Brother Lawrence's book.

I began praying silently for Wes. And an amazing thing happened. He leaned toward me and said, "You've got something
special in your life. I don't think I'm interested—at least not yet
—but I recognize it at work in your life."

Over the years I've had a lot of good experiences. And I keep
trying to keep myself in tune with Jesus Christ. I work at making closer and closer contact. I've worked out little ways to help.
For instance, there are several people I pray for every morning
as I shave and brush my teeth. I've been doing that now for at
least a year. It's become a habit to open up to the Lord as soon as
I turn the hot water on.

The second group comes as I get dressed and brush my shoes.
As I drive to my office, there's another list of people. I'm not
doing this perfectly, but I'm experiencing wonderful things as I
continue to make Christ a vital part of my daily world.

My friend Bruce has a similar idea. He told me recently, "I've
stopped playing my radio in the car. I found myself listening to
music I didn't really care about or talk shows I had no interest
in. Maybe I was avoiding the silence. Now I'm spending the time
in prayer. And it's been great so far."

Praying on the hoof offers no guarantee for spiritual growth.
But it holds out the potential. The quick prayers. The short con-
tacts with the Lord keep us turning back toward him.

I've long believed that what we fill our minds with determines
our attitude and our stance in life. A good example of this would
be my friend Gus. Gus and I started going to school together in
the same class in fifth grade. Gus was a reader. But he restricted
his reading to books on aviation—anything from biographies
of Amelia Earhart or the Wright brothers to novels like *Around
the World in Eighty Days* to autobiographical accounts like
Thirty Seconds over Tokyo. Gus attended movies—John Wayne
in *The Flying Tigers* or John Garfield in *Air Force*. By the time
we had reached high school, he could even recite statistics like

the number of planes manufactured in any year by Douglas Aircraft or Lockheed.

After high school Gus enlisted in the air force, eventually going into the field of aviation as a space engineer. He is a very knowledgeable fellow, although very limited in his likes and interests.

Gus used to make me angry at times. If I called him on the phone and said, "Hey, what're you doing?" he'd always reply, "Putting together a model of a B-17," or "Just reading the last issue of *Wings*." But I've always had a secret admiration for Gus. He made a decision early in life—he followed an area that interested him; he concentrated on that area. Slightly warped he might be, but he stuck at his field. I heard from him recently. He's still reading, thinking, dreaming, and living in his aerospace world. And he loves it.

That's the way I would like to be with God, and that's why praying on the hoof holds a fascination for me. I've always believed in set times for prayer—and I'll write about that in the next chapter. But praying on the hoof has some extra bonuses. It keeps calling us back into fellowship with Jesus Christ throughout the day when we're involved in other activities.

A friend of mine who is in the upper management bracket said, "The pressures in my job constantly try to squeeze out of me my sense of ethics and rightness. It would be easy to cut corners or wink at unfair practices. But I'd hate myself for all that afterwards."

What does he do to combat these problems?

"I've picked up several tricks to help me. Right outside my office is a drinking fountain. I always try to stop long enough for a quick sip—not because I need the water, but because it gives me a second to say, 'Jesus you're the water of life. Thanks.' Sometimes I offer a quick prayer about a real need or a problem I'm facing. I do a lot of dictating, and always pause for a few minutes before beginning to ask the Lord to clear my mind, to help me write letters with a spirit of fairness and honesty about them."

It also seems to me that praying on the hoof fits in with our fast-paced world. Maybe the stress of too much activity is killing us. Maybe we need to slow down. But the fact is, we do go at top-rate speed most of the time. So why not capitalize on that?

"Snatch a prayer," one friend says. I know what he means—a pause during the morning for a quick, heavenward reflection. These help remind us that we're God's children, and help fill our minds with Jesus Christ.

Last spring I conducted an overnight retreat for a local church. Our program centered around making prayer a practical reality. One of the concepts I worked with was praying on the hoof.

"That's a good idea, Mr. Murphey," several said. No one argued. I wondered, however, if any had decided to put the suggestions into practice.

Then I met Barbara at a social gathering some time later. She had attended the retreat and I had seen her only once or twice since that event. During our conversation she said, "By the way, Cec, remember when you taught us about being conscious of God during the day? It works. Honest."

Instead of saying "Of course it does," I held back and said, "Sounds like you've had a good experience with praying on the hoof."

"Sure have," she said.

I knew Barbara worked as a secretary for a firm of seven lawyers, and that they demanded complete accuracy. "I started in my job. When I'd sit down to transcribe a codicil or any legal paper, I'd find myself freezing up. I'd make all kinds of errors and have to start again. The Monday after our retreat, I put the paper in the machine and said, 'God, help me relax. Help me do an accurate job on this piece.' It came out perfect! Now I find myself praying almost every time I put paper in the machine. I'm not always 100 percent accurate, but I'll tell you one thing—I don't come home at night with tension headaches anymore!"

After a little more conversation Barbara said, "Why don't more people try it?"

I smiled and nodded. A good question. Why don't more people try praying on the hoof?

Questions for Thought
and Discussion

1. "Practicing the presence of God" is an old phrase. From page 22, what do you understand that term to mean?
2. Does praying on the hoof or practicing God's presence appeal to you? Have you ever tried this style of devotional life?
3. How do you feel about attempting to "pray on the hoof"? Could you remind yourself to pray? Constantly? How would you go about starting this "moment-by-moment relationship"?
4. Read the incident about my encounter with Wes (p. 23). Have you ever tried this when you're with a person you don't like? What do you think happened in this incident?
5. Gus (p. 23) narrowed his interests in life largely to one field. Can you think of how one might be really narrowed in on the Christian faith and yet avoid being tagged a person who's "so heavenly-minded that he's no earthly good"?
6. Recall experiences when you've found yourself "snatching a prayer." Was it an emergency need? A time of real problems?
7. Recall an experience when life seemed awfully good, and you paused merely to say "Thank you, Lord." How did you feel?
8. Does praying on the hoof seem to take the feeling out of prayer? Do you think it might become a mechanical kind of action?
9. Think of the advantages of praying on the hoof. Does this help bring God into more areas of your daily living? Can you be in prayer and yet aware of what's going on in the world around you?
10. Reflect on what life would be like for you if you constantly

prayed on the hoof. How would you see yourself? Describe
your relationships with other people, with your family,
your coworkers or employees.

11. For the next twenty-four hours, make an effort to think
about God in every conscious moment. If you're part of
a group study, report on your experiences.

12. "Pray constantly" (1 Thess. 5:17). How do you interpret
this verse? Does it say the same thing as praying on the
hoof or practicing the presence of God?

3
Hoofing—
A Second Look

I NEVER MET MARTHA WING ROBINSON, but I wish I had. People who knew her speak of her in the most venerated terms. To call her a woman of God sounds like a cliché. To say she always walked "in the spirit" rings of a distasteful piosity.

She ministered mostly in the Midwest and died in 1936. Outside of the ministers and missionaries with whom she worked, her name was not greatly known. But they have often referred to the unusual life and experience of this teacher to whom they owed so much. Their testimonies to her influence on their lives as well as some of her own writings have now been circulated around the world. Today, she's more widely known and carries a wider influence than she did forty years ago.

Her biographer wrote, "Martha Wing Robinson was used by God to blaze a trail, for others to follow, into the realm of God's complete possession of body and spirit where it is literally and actually true—not just figuratively or spiritually speaking—that it is 'Christ living in me.' Most fittingly, therefore, she has been called a trail blazer."

One of Mrs. Robinson's closest friends said, "One could not be in her presence long without recognizing that her life was controlled by the One who dwelt within her. There was an inner radiancy and something of a celestial fire which burned the love of Jesus into our very souls."

Another close associate wrote, "The outstanding thing about her was that Jesus had become the Center and All of her life

29

so that others have been impregnated with the same desire to
know Jesus and to have Him reigning with them, living out His
life so that both their personal lives and the meetings which they
might conduct would be controlled by Him." *

Even when allowances are made for the prejudice, loyalty, and
adulation of her devotees, the words sound like someone I've
never met. Someone I'd like to meet. Someone I'd like to be.

What would it be like, I've often wondered, to live a life in
total commitment to Jesus Christ. Praying constantly. Letting
nothing distract me. Letting nothing disturb perfect communion
and yet at the same time doing my work with utmost efficiency.

Not very realistic perhaps—a total commitment to Jesus
Christ and yet a productive, efficient life in the world. But it
could be done. I have really wanted it to become a reality in my
own life. What would it really be like to live "in the spirit"? I
have always understood that as living moment by moment—
every moment—in vital contact with the Holy Spirit.

At one time I even abandoned a set devotional time. After all,
as I trained myself constantly to turn to the Lord, to be always
in a spirit of prayer, why have a special time set aside for spiritual
contact? I'm not referring to stopping to pray about serious problems or emergencies, but the daily habit of getting into a quiet
spot and praying for people and needs.

Somehow I never quite lived up to that vision. But I really
tried. Some days went better than others, but over a period of at
least a year I realized I'd never fulfill the dream.

I used to think my problem was not having the spiritual
capacity of Martha Wing Robinson, Frank Laubach, or Brother
Lawrence. That may be true to an extent; certainly some people
have more of a mystic tendency than others. Realizing that we
all have different physical, spiritual, and emotional make-ups
helped me considerably; I learned there's no need to pattern my
life after Laubach or Robinson—just be the best Christian possible.

---

* All three quotes from Gordon P. Gardiner, *Radiant Glory* (Brooklyn:
Bread of Life Press), p. 4.

But no matter the reason, I finally realized that a prayer life fully "on the hoof" wasn't for me. In rethinking this, I realize several reasons why:

First, *my prayer life became more superficial* when I prayed only on the hoof. In terms of quantity, I'm not sure whether I prayed more or less. Probably my prayers covered a greater area. I made a concerted effort to be aware of God's presence all the time. I talked with Jesus Christ while sipping midmorning coffee, or while walking to the post office in the afternoon.

Yet, for all the frequency of my prayer, something wasn't quite right. I covered the territory, but had no sense of any in-depth praying. My prayers consisted mainly of "help," "guide," "encourage," "convert"—followed by a name. Or, if I tuned in on praise, it was largely, "Thank you for. . . ."

Nothing wrong with this style. *But is that all?* It was like pecking my wife on the lips before leaving for the office in the morning as compared to a passionate embrace. The peck was better than nothing, but couldn't I have an experience like the passionate embrace more frequently? I never quite learned the secret of the spiritual giants—and perhaps that's why *they* are the spiritual giants!

Second, *I missed a closeness with Christ.* There's something significant about being alone, in a quiet spot, with no one but Jesus Christ. My hands doing nothing, my body fairly well relaxed—I talk to him, but he also talks to me. Or sometimes it's not even a conscious talking—just a togetherness.

Seven years ago I suddenly began vomiting blood, passed out, and woke up on the way to the hospital. At the time I had no idea how serious my condition was. Both on the rapid trip and after arriving at the hospital, I felt a closeness to Jesus Christ. I didn't feel like talking, because my body was weak, but I had a kind of glow inside.

Later I learned that I had frightened my wife because she had thought I was going to die. As I lay there in the room, I kept saying to her, "Honey, I feel so close to the Lord." I've missed that kind of closeness in my praying on the hoof. That time when the Lord and his child are quiet and warm in each other's presence is important to me.

A third problem with praying on the hoof: *my concentration was often diverted.* I would watch the red light while I was asking God to reconcile Paul and Susan. Surely God hears my intercessory prayers while I stand in the check-out line at K-Mart, or as I carry the plastic garbage bag outside. But there is also the need for times of full concentration. Some needs can't be handled lightly.

Jesus himself must have felt that way. Before calling Lazarus from the dead, he said, "Father, I thank thee that thou hast heard me. I knew that thou hearest me always, but I have said this on account of the people standing by, that they may believe that thou didst send me" (John 11:41–42). I don't want to read too much into that verse, but I assume he meant that he was in perpetual communion with the Father, and that he was praying audibly only for the benefit of those around. And yet at least twice in the Gospels it is recorded that he went away to pray by himself (Mark 1:36; Luke 11:1).

I began praying for Judi and Bill in September. I felt they had gifts from the Lord and could be wonderfully used with our teenagers. I began praying for them—hoof-type prayers. They were among those I prayed for each morning as I walked to the post office to pick up mail.

In early November my concern for them increased. Whenever I mentioned their names in prayer, I felt that a touch-and-let-go prayer wasn't enough. "Lord, lead Judi and Bill ..." and the burden was there. It continued several days.

So in the morning, before shaving or getting dressed, I began praying in a quiet place. Judi and Bill stayed at the top of my list. Two weeks later, they came to me. "We'd like to offer ourselves to do youth work and be used any way you think we can fit in."

We rejoiced together. And I knew that my concerted prayer on their behalf had been directed by the Lord.

A fourth problem for me with praying on the hoof was that

my praying tended to depend on my emotional swings. I re-member how that worked in one single day. That morning I received a telephone call that my first book * had been accepted for publication. My heart gushed in spontaneous praise. Constant pauses during the morning to worship God. To thank him. To pray for friends. To ask his guidance. A memorable morning!

At noon I went to the post office to pick up my mail. Among the two dozen items of mail, five separate rejections stared at me—four articles and one book manuscript!

"God, I thought you called me to write. Look at this—five rejections."

Returning to my office, I buried myself in other activities. When I left late that afternoon to make a call at the hospital, I realized with sudden clarity that I hadn't prayed on the hoof all afternoon.

"I'm just too low to think about prayer," I muttered to myself. Perhaps I actually needed prayer even more—but it didn't work that way.

Several later occasions confirmed this attitude. It was always easier to pray when things went well. Or when an emergency situation occurred. But when life took one of its downward cycles, prayer seemed a relatively unimportant part of my life.

I never stopped praying completely—even when going through low emotional periods. In fact, those next-to-nothing prayer days forced me to rethink how important prayer is to the Christian. And if prayer is important, establishing and maintaining the *habit* of prayer is equally important!

When my grandson Danny was nearly two, he entered the stage of making sure everything followed a specific pattern. For instance, he usually ate Sunday dinner with us. Before we prayed, he would look around the table to make certain every-one had hands folded and eyes closed. If one of us didn't, he let out a barrage of noise that said (although we weren't always certain of his words), "Put those hands together so we can pray!"

---

* *Prayer: Pitfalls and Possibilities* (New York: Hawthorn Books, 1975).

Then we were ready. It was a habit for Danny. But it's a habit he learned by constant repetition. His parents had taught him that he did not begin eating until after they paused for prayer. He may not have understood all the ritual, but he did understand the action that took place first.

This incident with Danny reminds me of the significance of habits. They can work for us as well as against us! Even on days when I don't feel like praying, I do. My alarm goes off, and perhaps on those days I don't leap from bed—it's more like a turtle-speed crawl. But somewhere between shaving, breakfast, and leaving for the office, I have my devotional time. It wouldn't seem right for me not to have that time—even if I have to cut the reading or the praying short. I may have to fight the problem of my mind wandering (with which I deal in a later chapter), but I *do* pray. It's much like Danny insisting we all bow our heads and close our eyes—it's part of the habit. It belongs to my pattern of life.

This chapter has largely sounded as though praying on the hoof has little value. That's not true in my life. I'm constantly reaching toward a greater awareness of God's presence, trying to actualize in my life his "Lo, I am with you always"—not that I believe Jesus comes and goes, but my awareness of him does.

I believe in praying on the hoof. I also firmly believe in having set times. In fact, I'm excited about the combination of the two. It doesn't have to be either/or. Perhaps Brother Lawrence, being a lay monk, living in a religious atmosphere and being by nature more attuned toward the mystical life, reached a greater plane of relationship. I confess I'd like to have that sense of being every moment in the presence of the Lord.

Praying on the hoof is just one of those means toward a goal!

Questions for Thought
and Discussion

1. Even making allowances for the prejudice of her devotees, what kind of woman do you think Martha Wing Robinson was? Would you have been comfortable around her? Would you have liked her?
2. Have you ever been in the presence of someone and felt that person was fully controlled at that moment by the Spirit of God? If so, describe that person and how you felt.
3. What would it require for Jesus to become "the Center and All" of your life so that others who came into contact with you would have a compelling desire to follow Christ? Would you like that kind of relationship with Christ?
4. In this chapter, I contrast praying on the hoof with having a set devotional time. If you had to make a choice between the two, which would you choose? Why?
5. I listed four weaknesses in praying on the hoof. Do you agree with each of them? Can you think of additional ones?
6. In prayer, which do you think (generally) is more important—making requests or being in close fellowship with Christ?
7. How much do your emotional swings affect your prayer life? How faithful are you when you're tired? Slightly ill? Feeling on top?
8. Jesus went away to pray by himself (Mark 1:35; Luke 11:1; Luke 5:16). How important was that for Jesus? Do these verses imply that we also need to get away from the crowd and pray?
9. Can you recall an incident when you were with several people and felt the need to get away, either to pray or to clear your own thinking? How important did it seem to you? If you actually got away, how did you feel afterwards?
10. Jesus said, "Lo, I am with you always" (Matt. 28:20). We

find the promise, "I will never fail you nor forsake you" in
Hebrews 13:5. How does praying on the hoof remind you
of these promises?

4

Getting Started
and Staying Going

EIGHT PEOPLE KNELT in front of the rest of us, asking us to pray for them. Each had vocalized the same concern: a desire for a consistent devotional life. And by consistent they meant one that put God into the picture every day through prayer and Bible reading.

By four months later, I'd talked casually with most of the group. Six of them said that they had been able to maintain their commitment.

As I talked with them, and as I examined my own prayer life, I realized that consistent praying doesn't just happen. It's planned for. We plan for success.

My friend Tony is a man of many beginnings; he'll tell you so himself. He starts new projects every week—always a new gimmick, a new appliance or convenience. But he also drops projects just as quickly as he starts. So it's not enough merely to get going initially; it is necessary to sustain the commitment.

In this chapter I suggest some ways to help you get started in a daily time and also to help you keep going:

First, *get up!* Don't lie in bed thinking about how you ought to pray. Don't lie there in the comfort of warm bedclothes and say, "Three more minutes" or "I'll start tomorrow."

Here's something that has worked for me. When I suspect that I'm going to have trouble getting up and getting started the next morning, I pray the night before! "Lord, I know you can help me get up when the alarm goes off." On those occasions I visualize myself jumping from bed and starting the day with new vigor. Strange, but when I envision myself doing that, and as I ask the Lord to make it possible, I find I can get up more easily!

Getting up at a certain time or going to sleep at night are matters of established habit. And we may have to take drastic action to break up those encrusted habits. Years ago I had a terrible time with the alarm clock; I could shut it off, stuff it under my pillow, and return to sleep. Then, in order to break that habit, I placed the clock on a table on the far side of the room. As soon as that alarm started, I jumped from bed and ran to shut it off. By the sheer act of leaping from the bed and bounding across the room, I was suddenly awake. Then I could stay up.

You're not going to get up tomorrow morning unless you determine tonight that you'll do it. Commit yourself to God. Tell yourself you're going to get up. Tell God and ask his help. Then you'll do it!

Second, *remind yourself* that we grow spiritually through prayer and Bible reading (see my chapter on means of grace, "Prayer—Cause and Effect?"). You may need to pray frequently, "Lord, I need to grow. Make me want to grow." If you faithfully ask that way, my guess is that you'll soon start making preparations to carry out your prayers!

Third, *start small*. Don't try to be a spiritual giant in one leap of faith. In the beginning (and even after you mature), it's not length of time, but consistency, that counts.

Last fall, my wife and I began jogging together. I had been going regularly to the health spa for some time, but it was a new activity for her. So we began at her pace. The first morning we got up earlier than usual and jogged exactly four-tenths of a mile (we had marked off the tenths of a mile on the street near our home). Within a few days we were up to half a mile. Then we escalated to seven-tenths.

I recall the first morning we completed a mile together. It took us nearly fourteen minutes, which is a little slow, but we were so delighted to have accomplished the feat we didn't worry about how long it took. On subsequent mornings, we knocked the time down to less than ten minutes. Now when we jog it's hard to think that we once found it difficult to run half a mile.

That's the way to develop the habit of prayer and devotion. Start small and work forward. Aim for five minutes in the beginning—or even three. Set up a prayer list of ten people or concerns. Don't try to pray for every single person you know. Or don't make the mistake of just rattling off names to God. Take each concern and pray specifically.

I suggest to folks that they not think about establishing a prayer life for all the days they'll live on the earth. Initially determine to be faithful for one full week. Not ten years or two months, but one week. As you complete that first week, you will have incentive to try for week two. And once a habit has been firmly entrenched, you expand your goals. From trying for one week, you might say, "I know I can do it for a full month." (I'll talk about failures and breakdowns later.)

As I mentioned in the previous chapter, my three-year-old grandson eats Sunday dinner with us almost every week. His dad usually puts food on the boy's plate. Little Danny's always saying, "I want more of that, Daddy. Give me more." But his dad's aware that desire is often bigger than ability. He calmly replies, "Eat this and then you'll get more." And frequently Danny says, even before he's eaten everything on his plate, "I'm finish. Get down now?"

Lesson: Don't be too spiritually ambitious at first.

Fourth, *use devotional aids* to get started. Some of the most difficult questions about establishing a prayer habit are: What do I say? How do I get started? What part of the Bible do I read?

Most denominations publish a devotional guide (usually monthly). A number of independent companies such as *Our Daily Bread* also publish these guides, which consist of a selected Bible reading, a brief interpretation and application of the verses, and a concluding prayer.

I think, for many people, these are good *starting* places. My friend Dale says it helps her get into the mood for prayer. Ralph told me that it gets him thinking in a particular vein. For instance, if the lesson for the day is about foreign missions or about social action, Ralph starts by praying for those needs.

Personally, I don't use devotional aids. I prefer to do my reading by going through books of the Bible—sometimes reading one whole book at a sitting. Occasionally, I'll depart from my straight Bible reading, and use a commentary as a devotional guide in going through a book. This nearly always gives me insight into a difficult passage that I might not otherwise grasp. I find that this is especially true when going through the Old Testament prophets.

Fourth, *accept failures*. They're going to happen—even to the spiritual veterans. We all have unforeseen problems hitting us, or ill health preventing us.

This morning, for instance, I had no Bible reading and only a brief time of prayer. Reason: I slept late. For several nights I had been out visiting people in our church as well as attending and conducting worship services. I nearly always start my day early, and this past week I was ending my days very late. This morning I was simply too tired to have my regular worship time.

I don't feel guilty about it. However, if I let it slide two days or three—then I'd feel guilty. And I'd also miss the intimacy with the Lord. I like to think of my prayer time as a daily occasion of loving fellowship with my best friend. He doesn't expect me to go beyond my physical endurance. He doesn't feel cheated when I'm too tired or too sick to read and pray.

This morning as I had my brief minutes of prayer (and then did my praying on the hoof while getting ready to leave for the office), I recall saying, "Thanks, Lord, for allowing me to sleep and to feel so rested."

I can pray that way because I believe the Lord wants me to get rest and to be at my best for his service. And if there was any loss, it was my loss—my lack of opportunity for spiritual grace.

Fifth, *tell someone* about your devotional commitment. Strange, but that seems one of the best ways I know to keep myself faithful in any commitment I make.

Three years ago, after looking at myself sideways and full view in the large bathroom mirrors in my house, as well as having one of my daughters tease me about the football I had hidden under my shirt, I decided to lose weight. After carefully thinking it through I set my goal at losing twenty-five pounds *and* keeping it off. Keeping it off meant giving serious thought to my whole eating pattern.

In three months I had lost the weight. In the three years since I have kept off the weight consistently. By that I mean that I regularly gain two or three pounds, then lose them. I refuse to allow myself to exceed my ideal weight by more than five pounds.

Part of the reason for my success is that I told all my friends about my plans—in fact, for awhile I believe I told anyone who would listen. I'm sure people got tired of hearing about how many calories an apple contains or how many calories a person can burn off by one hour of moderate exercise.

But it worked! People didn't ask, "How's the diet doing?" Instead, they said, "Hey, you've really lost weight, haven't you?"

The same idea works with the devotional commitment. Tell several of your friends what you're trying to do. You might even ask them to check up on you from time to time. I'm sure that's one reason groups like TOPS and Weight Watchers are so successful—people have to weigh in at each meeting!

The other day a friend of mine spoke about *positive* addiction. That's a good way to think about our devotional life. We want to become addicted to the habit of consistent, daily time with Jesus Christ. We feel our best when we've had it, and somehow our days don't go quite right when we don't. Because I believe I *need* prayer and the reading of the Bible every day in order to grow in my spiritual commitment, I also believe in using any legitimate means to help me reach and maintain these goals.

The other night in a sharing group, Joe said in his hesitant way, "I can't believe what's happened to me in the last year. I never thought I'd be a person who reads and prays every day. Not *every* day! But I do and I really feel good about it. In fact, when I don't have my prayer time before going to work I'm not quite right for the day. It's like someone who always eats a big breakfast having to rush out of the house with only a piece of toast and a cup of coffee."

Joe got into the prayer habit eight months ago. And he's determined to keep it going. Perhaps that's the biggest reason of all for his consistency—he's *determined*.

I hope you'll start forming the habit of daily fellowship with Christ. Why not start today? Maybe even right now. Mark off three minutes of time and tell yourself, "Every day this week I'm going to give the Lord three minutes of my time—three minutes with no interruptions." Who knows? You may soon up that to five minutes. Or ten. You might just become absolutely and positively addicted to fellowship with Jesus Christ!

Questions for Thought
and Discussion

1. Many people have trouble getting started on a regular time of prayer and Bible study. Look over the suggestions in this chapter. Which ones do you find helpful to you and your situation?

2. Reflect on your own failures to pray consistently. What frequent problems do you encounter? What kind of practical steps could you take to change from failure to success?

3. The third suggestion is *start small*. If you're not regularly setting aside time for prayer every day, make a commitment to yourself (and to the others if you're in a group) to begin a daily time with the Lord. Say to the others, "I pledge that, for the next week, I'm going to spend _____ minutes in prayer and Bible reading every day." The next time you meet together, report on your success.

4. The chapter suggests telling someone of your commitment. How can this help you?

5. Tony starts projects almost daily and seldom finishes any of them. What kind of help can you offer someone like Tony?

6. If you have trouble getting out of bed in the morning, try preparing yourself the night before. Determine to get up when the alarm goes off. Can you think of anything to help you so you won't snap off the alarm and return to sleep?

7. Have you ever used devotional aids on a regular basis? Any in your group might share their experiences. You might want to obtain such materials and try them for two weeks. At the end of that time, ask yourself questions such as, Did it stimulate more or better prayer? Did the material help me pray more effectively? Did it help me focus my prayer concerns?

8. We form habits by repeating action. Determine each day to pray, "Lord, help me develop a consistent devotional life."

Ask for the Lord's help in the troubled areas. If you're part of a group, stop now and have an informal time of prayer. Go around the room and have anyone who wishes vocalize briefly in prayer his or her problem. Close with a request for God's help.

9. Perhaps you'd like to keep a weekly record of your devotional time. Record the date and note whether or not you were successful. Sometimes looking back over our record of failures and successes can make us try harder. If you discover that your failure rate exceeds your success rate, read the chapter again. Then share with the group or a friend, asking special prayer for yourself.

5
The Wandering Mind

TUESDAY I DID MY DEVOTIONAL READING in the book of Judges. It's a familiar book to me—especially the chapters about Samson. After twenty minutes I looked up from the pages and realized something: I had been reading, but couldn't recall a single thing I had just read!

That's not the first time it's happened—and I imagine I'll have regular occurrences of the problem. The first time I remember it happening to me was only a few months after my conversion. I had gone outside for my devotional time. It was one of those surprisingly warm mornings in late spring. I leaned back in my chair and began praying.

I thanked the Lord for the world he had given me to enjoy— the budding trees, the warmth, even the birds fluttering in the apple tree. Watching the birds soar upward, I thought of the way planes fly. That reminded me that I had been on a plane only a few months earlier. But the weather had been, as the pilot said, "turbulent," and despite his best efforts and our seat belts, the two-hour trip had been bumpy and uncomfortable. The discomfort in that plane reminded me of the time the Navy sent me from Chicago to Maryland by train . . .

My mind snapped back to the present. It had been wandering off into the clouds. One thought had triggered another, and that had kept the thoughts flowing on and on—getting farther and farther away from my devotional time with Jesus Christ.

"Lord, forgive me for allowing my mind to wander like that."

I felt so ashamed. I even promised I'd not let it happen again. But it did happen again—many times. And even now, after more than twenty years of being a follower of Jesus Christ, I still have occasional problems with my mind wandering.

For instance, during my devotions the other day, I was praying for Julie. "Lord, she's specifically asked me to pray about her weight and her compulsive eating. Help Julie . . ." I imagined Julie standing in front of me with her expansive stomach. Like Ralph, who's nearly fifty pounds overweight. But Ralph wasn't always like that. I remember when he was thinner than I am . . . A lot of his problem is that his wife likes to cook too much and is always urging him to have a second (or even a third!) piece of cake . . .

"There I go again." I snapped back to Julie. Then on to the next person for whom I wanted to pray.

It happens to all of us, and it happens frequently! Rather than deplore the fact, I thank God for the wonderful minds he created in us. We don't merely focus on a subject and remain fixed on it indefinitely. Even when we're concentrating with the deepest intensity, our minds flit from one thought to another. We can control those jumps. We can prevent our minds from moving in a capricious fashion by channeling our thoughts. But we can't stop the motion!

Until that fact became clear, I constantly berated myself. "Lord, I've allowed something to crowd you out of my mind. I've allowed something of lesser value and importance to push you out of the way." Now I've taken another approach. When I catch my mind wandering, I take corrective measures. Over the past few years several ideas have helped me combat the problem of the wandering mind:

First, *I keep a pencil and pad handy when I pray.* A frequent problem for me is for a thought like "Don't forget to pick up the cleaning today" or "Write a letter to your mother" to slip into my mind. Those intrusions could easily stop my whole devotional time. Now I reach over, jot down the items that occurred to me, and return to my praying. The thought is only a momentary interruption.

Second, *I try to reserve the same time and same place for prayer*. We're all creatures of habit. Once we establish a room and a time for prayer, we find ourselves getting into the routine.

One of the breakthroughs for overweight people has been the concept of behavior modification. The advocates stress that a person should use one place and only one place for eating. They say, "Don't poke food into your mouth while you're standing. Don't munch while staring at the TV. Eat at the table, seated, and finish your meal without jumping up and down getting extra food."

The same principle can work for prayer life. Maintaining a certain time and place for prayer creates an atmosphere for a devotional life. While I believe we can pray anywhere, in my normal routine there are special places where I pray. I've consciously made each of them a habit so that the minute I'm in that place, my mind turns to Jesus Christ.

For instance, my wife and I jog in the mornings at 5:30. As soon as my feet start making the paces, I'm silently praying. The habit has been consciously formed so that now it becomes almost automatic for me.

Try developing a devotional habit yourself. Kneel beside your bed. Or sit upright in a chair; the place isn't as important as making it part of a daily routine. But *my* favorite place is kneeling beside my bed. Perhaps it's the habit of years of repeating the same posture. At any rate, the very act of kneeling seems to put my mind into the attitude of prayer..

Third, *make out a prayer list*. This has become a necessity for me. I keep my list in front of me, and it helps pull me back to the subject when my mind begins to wander.

Some days I don't even glance at the list—no need to. Other days I don't pray for everyone on my list. Occasions arise when I'm so burdened for a need that I spend my devotional time praying only for that one person or concern. But I keep the list handy. And I change the list every four or five weeks. If I don't, my prayer time tends to become a routine of going down a list and requesting spiritual blessings for Christian friends and salvation for non-Christians.

Fourth, *try singing*. The Psalms are Jewish hymns. I often
make up my own tunes and sing quietly. I wouldn't want anyone else to hear me—I'm not singing for them anyway. I can
put one line into a minor key and then switch to a major and
jump up and down the scale. Or occasionally I'll take a familiar
tune and fit the words into that meter. That's all part of my
worship. I refuse to have my private time with Jesus Christ destroyed because of a wandering mind.

Fifth, and this refers more to Bible reading than strictly praying, *read faster*. Surprisingly, I've discovered that when I attempt
to read the Bible in what one might call a devout speed (i.e., one
word at a time), my wandering increases!

For example, I read between six and eight pages in twenty
minutes. I usually look at the clock when I start (I have this
life-long habit of timing almost everything!). If, upon glancing
up after two pages I discover that I've used ten minutes, I know
I'm dragging and my mind is wandering. So I move faster.

Sixth, *pray aloud*. It's much like singing. If you are too in-
hibited to try the musical trip, why not talk to the Lord out loud?
Or even read your Bible out loud.

My friend Patsy says she does half her reading this way. She's
a night person by nature, but discovered that the only way she
could get Bible reading and praying done was to get up earlier
in the morning. "And it takes me an hour to get fully awake!"
she added. So she helps herself by doing two things: (1) She
prays and reads aloud. (2) She keeps a wet washcloth handy,
and if her eyelids get heavy, she wipes her face and goes on.

"At times it almost seems like cruel and unusual punishment,
but when it's over, I'm so glad I stuck it out. Having that time
with the Lord makes the rest of my day go so much better."

Seventh, *try different translations*. Most years I read the Bible
through twice. Because of this life-long habit, it's easy to skip
over what I'm reading. After all, how many of us reread books?
I'm an avid reader, and yet I recall reading very few books more
than once. The second time through bores me—I know everything that's coming.

But the Bible's different. I really believe God gives us spiritual strength through the reading of that book. So I keep reading. And I use different versions of the Bible to help me keep my mind on what I'm reading. For the past few years I have read two translations at the same time. For instance, I'll read the New Testament in the Revised Standard Version at the same time I'm reading the Old Testament in the Jerusalem Bible.

I have no complete answers to the problem of the wandering mind. But I'm aware of two things. First, it happens to all of us. Second, we can set up habits and devices to aid us when our minds start to wander. I've shared a few of my "secrets" to combat this problem. Give it a try; you may discover a few secrets of your own.

Questions for Thought
and Discussion

1. If in the past few weeks you've had an experience with your mind wandering during your devotional time, share it with the others. How did you cope?
2. What kind of feelings do you have when you go through a period of inability to concentrate? Guilt? Discouragement? Disgust with yourself? An attitude of "tomorrow it will be better"?
3. Read the seven suggestions offered in this chapter. Think of each one. Which ones do you think will be especially helpful? Which ones are you going to try yourself?
4. Can you understand why the second suggestion ("Same time, same place") is important? Do you think it's easier to pray in a familiar surrounding?
5. Suggestion number six is to pray aloud. Have you tried this? How would this help keep the mind from wandering?
6. In the past, what have you done when you've not been able to concentrate on reading the Bible?
7. Reread the first paragraph of this chapter. Has such an experience ever happened to you? Perhaps you weren't particularly conscious of your mind wandering, but after a passage of time you realized you weren't involved in what you were doing. How did you feel? What did you do about it?
8. Suggestion three involves using a prayer list. Have you ever tried one? If so, share your experience with the others.
9. Whether or not you've ever used a prayer list, try one for the next month. Then ask yourself, "Has it helped my concentration?" At the end of one month, share your experiences with the group.
10. Have you discovered any helps, other than the ones men-

tioned? Can you think of any not mentioned that could be useful?

6

Spiritual Biorhythms

SINCE 1972 I'VE KEPT a reflective journal in which I write my thoughts and feelings about what's currently going on in my life. Sometimes I address God; other times I direct questions to myself or to an imaginary third person.

Here's an entry for September 13, 1976:

> Ever feel as though you don't want to pray? I've been feeling that way for several weeks. In fact, in some ways I'm at the lowest spiritual point that I've plummeted to in at least fifteen years. On a feeling level, I'm simply numb.
>
> I'm not discouraged or depressed. I've learned to accept that these things happen. While I'm not giving up, I sure hope this low period doesn't last long.

On October 1, I concluded my journal entry with this:

> What a productive week so far! Seem to have so much pep. My writing almost flows out of me so that my fingers on the typewriter can't quite keep up with my thoughts.

As I look back at those two entries as well as several others, I realize how my moods have swung between high and low. The uplifts make life exciting, but the low periods are hard to accept. I've been swinging up and down for a long time.

So much of my early teaching assured me of living continu-

ously on the mountaintop because I had surrendered to Christ.
But no one lives on the mountain—they only visit there.

My first spiritual low hit me nearly three years after my conversion. The constant and enthusiastic joy evaporated. The forward push lost its impetus. Stagnation set in.

How did I cope then? I tried harder, determined that sin in
my life must be keeping me away from God. I searched my
heart. I sent up prayers, asking forgiveness for every conceivable
sin I might have accidentally committed. Instead of my daily
Bible reading of twenty or thirty minutes, I read forty-five minutes, even though my mind wandered or I felt sluggish after
only five. I tried subvocalizing my reading, then other things
such as switching versions of the Bible. For a while I read a devotional commentary along with my Bible. Nothing worked;
nothing pulled me out of my slump.

I put more effort in pulling myself up spiritually. If there was
no sin, then the devil was trying to keep me from praying and
studying. I began having my devotions out loud more often. So
that I wouldn't awaken Shirley, I went into the back of the
house. Several mornings I walked outside. My mind continually
wandered, but I stuck with it.

After several months, I felt as though I had tried long enough.
"God, there's no sense of your presence in my life. Where's the
joy which is supposed to characterize Christians? What happened to the peace you promised? Others may have it, but I
don't."

During that time two of my friends experienced a renewal
and seemed to bubble over with enthusiasm. I became sharply
aware of the contrast in our lives. That disheartened me even
more.

One afternoon in late winter I walked down the street, feeling
discouraged. I had been on this spiritual downgrade since early
fall. "God, why don't you do something for me?" I prayed
again and again.

That year had produced a severe winter. In northern Illinois,
where we lived, snow never really melted before another blanket

covered us. I had heard on the radio the day before that we had an accumulation of twenty inches of snow. Several times I almost slipped on the icy pavements. I wondered whether the snow would ever melt, if spring would ever come again.

Then something caught my attention. I almost missed it, but its bright green color contrasted with the dingy white all around. A tiny plant had pushed itself through the snow. The sun overhead had only half-heartedly attempted to melt the white mass. But there was the green growth. I didn't know if it was a weed, a flower, or a sapling. But it was *alive*. It had survived the coldness, darkness, and harshness of the elements. Snow and cold temperatures wouldn't defeat that hardy plant.

Bending down, I touched its leaves. I wanted to pull it up by the roots and shout to everyone, "Look! Look!" And in that moment I knew that I, too, would make it. I could push through the deadening forces in my life. I would survive.

Within a week, a sense of renewed spiritual energy flowed through me. There may have been physiological causes for my down-and-up streak. Perhaps someone could have provided a psychological explanation. I *do* know that a renewal took place, and that I was on the spiritual climb once again.

I've discovered that the spiritual path isn't always easy. It's not a continual upward movement. My wife used to sing a country-type hymn: "It's not an easy road we're traveling." That song reminds me of an experience at a ministers' retreat in 1972. On the first evening, each person received a sheet of paper, a crayon, and instructions to "draw a graph showing your spiritual journey."

I had always envisioned the spiritual journey as an ascending line. But as I thought about *my life,* I realized it had peaks, followed by downward movements. I recalled the spurt of growth after my conversion, another one during the months when Shirley and I dated and involved ourselves in a myriad of Christian activities, another when I first went to Africa as a missionary. Then I thought of the low spots. There was a bad time in 1959, and another low spot in 1967 when, after six years of missionary

service, we found ourselves physically and spiritually depleted.
At that retreat several ministers shared their graphs. Some of
them varied far more than mine!

God promises his victory for his people. However, we don't
possess these gifts every moment. They come and go. They are
part of the experience of God's grace at work in us. Our ups and
downs of living have been the subject of a lot of research in recent years. A popular theory is called *biorhythm.*

The idea of biorhythms is that we all have a natural cycle.
Several interesting facts have come out of research. For instance,
golfer Arnold Palmer won the British Open Golf Tournament
in July 1962. A study of his biorhythm chart showed that he was
high in all three areas measured—physical, emotional, and intellectual. Two weeks later, a triple low period, he lost the P.G.A.
Tournament. Mark Spitz, Olympic superstar winner of seven
gold medals, including setting new swimming records, had
cycles of high in both physical and emotional areas during the
1972 events in Munich.

Significant research has involved investigating the cycles of
pilots of airline crashes. For instance, Robert Loft, who was pilot
of the Eastern Airlines giant Lockheed L-1011 TriStar Jet with
176 on board, crashed over the Florida Everglades on December
29, 1972. A chart of Captain Loft's biorhythm cycle showed him
at an intellectual low, and almost as low on the physical cycle.
Don Jonz, who flew the Cessna C110C that crashed with Con-
gressman Hale Boggs on board in Alaska on October 6, 1972,
had a biorhythm nearing bottom on both physical and emotional, and had already hit the lowest point on the intellectual.

I am not advocating that people become devotees of biorhythm. I include this because it may be a tool to help us understand why we don't remain constant. This may help explain
why we have our spiritual swings. I know there is a natural
rhythm to our moods and feelings. And I'm learning to accept
that in myself.

Friday of last week I tried reading my Bible as usual. It took a
great deal of effort to keep my mind on the text. I finally laid it

aside and said, "Lord, my mind is sluggish today. I'm just going to lie here and concentrate on you and pray for the needs of my friends." I spent half my devotional time in prayer before I fell asleep.

Later I thought over my week. I had been up early every morning and never been in bed before eleven—averaging six hours of sleep a night. No wonder I felt sluggish! Other times I've not really been able to account for my down-moods. Even so, I don't get upset. I simply say, "Father, I can't cut it today. I'm tired" (or "I'm bored" or "I'm just sluggish"). And I know it's okay.

In the early 1970s, I went through a difficult time in my life. There were a lot of problems in the church where I pastored. Our community became a transitional neighborhood, and most of our members moved away. In reality, I went through a period of depression over the situation—although I didn't think of it as depression. My symptom was constant sluggishness. I wanted to sleep—ten hours a day wasn't unusual. Once I slept nearly fourteen hours; I could never remember doing that before! As the problems found solutions, and decisions were made, my energy surfaced again. Within a few days I was back into the normal swing of life.

I've written this chapter because we need to realize that's the way the spiritual life operates. We constantly flow between ups and downs, fruitfulness and dormancy.

When we first moved to Atlanta we had a pecan tree in our yard. That fall it bore abundantly, and we could hardly collect all the precious nuts. The next year the tree appeared almost barren. We were worried, but a neighbor laughed, "You'll get a good crop again next year. The pecan tree needs a fallow season. Every other year you get a good crop."

That's helped me understand myself and my world. We all have our fallow times. In the Old Testament, God told the people to plant for six years. But in the seventh year—the sabbath—the ground was not to be plowed or planted. The eighth year they started the process again. Later those Jews went into slavery. One of the things God said was that they would stay seventy years—the number of the sabbath years they had planted their crops and not left the ground fallow.

That's the first rule about the spiritual life: no one—absolutely no one—walks every moment of every day in top spiritual form.

Second, our down spots are temporary. That fact encourages me. I think of the wit who said his favorite passage from the Bible was, "And it came to pass." He added, "Thanks be to God it didn't come to stay!" When I find myself hitting a low period, I'm learning to say, "Okay, Lord. I'll take the low road today. You'll soon put me on the high road again, won't you?"

Accepting the facts isn't enough. We don't have to say, "When God stirs me up I'll pray again . . . or read my Bible . . . or work for him." Accepting doesn't mean giving up. It means admitting, "That's the way things are." The next step is, "Now here's what I plan to do about it."

I know that some days I don't operate at full potential in my job, but I operate anyway. One morning my then thirteen-year-old daughter said, "Daddy, I'm sure dreading going to school today. I have a test in math, and I'm not even sure what's going on in the class." Before I had a chance to respond, she added, "But I'm going. I just hate the thought of going."

It's that way for everybody on some days. Maturing in our Christian experience often demands of us, "Keep moving ahead; keep trying," when we simply don't feel like going on. It helps to know ups and downs are natural parts of our Christian journey.

Questions for Thought and Discussion

1. Can you see how knowing about biorhythms could be helpful in dealing with day-to-day situations? Can you think of any serious dangers in relying upon such information? Would it bother you to investigate biorhythm?
2. Can you agree that we all have *natural* cycles of ups and downs? Do you know of any measures (outside of drugs) which can alter such changes? Is the best solution simply to accept them as they come?
3. If you were to draw a picture of your spiritual journey, what would it look like? Share this with the others. You may actually want to take pen and paper and do this.
4. Can you look at natural reasons (other than cyclical) which explain ups and downs? Lack of sufficient sleep? Type of diet? Amount of exercise? Pressure in our work? Unexpected events which either promote good feelings or bring sorrow?
5. On days when you're not operating at your full potential, how do you feel about yourself? Good? Angry? Self-deprecating?
6. On page 57, I compare life to the fruitfulness of the pecan tree. Do you think that's a good analogy? Do you have periods when you're more fruitful, happier, healthier, more alert than other periods of time?
7. Can you think of a long period when you were on the low level, such as that described on page 54? If so, share some of your feelings.
8. On page 58, there is the statement, "No one—absolutely no one—walks every moment of every day in top spiritual form." Explain why you agree or disagree.
9. Try keeping a journal or diary for the next five weeks. Each day when you have your devotional time, write down

your feelings. Are you on a line of ascendancy? A downward fall? After five weeks, try to chart your spiritual
temperature for that period.

7

Let's Give Account

It's EASY TO LIKE James Martin. He's in his early thirties—tall, dark, extremely good-looking, with shoulders like a quarterback. But it's his boyish grin and open face that grab you. His candor strikes you almost from the start. James has a sharp perception of his strengths, and just as readily acknowledges his weaknesses. When you talk to him, you can tell by the expression on his face that he actually listens.

I met James through the local chaplains' association. We are both ordained ministers in different denominations, but we established an immediate rapport. We set up a luncheon appointment for the following week so we could get better acquainted. That day we picked at our food as we found ourselves easily opening up and sharing our spiritual journeys with each other.

Both of us had recently moved into the area. Neither of us had yet established any deep relationships on a peer level. I had only recently left a weekly sharing group. A minister with whom I had been close had moved more than three hundred miles north. For several months I had lacked a prayer partner. During our conversation I expressed to James the kind of need I felt. He expressed a similar need. We arranged to meet the following week in my office.

That Tuesday we talked a few minutes about prayer and about our specific needs. Then James startled me with a sentence I would think over many times and continue coming back to: "I need someone to be accountable to."

My initial reaction was negative. Oh no, I thought—those Lutherans with their forms and their guilt. And another helping of guilt I don't need. I was beginning to think I had made a mistake with James.

"You see, Cec, I tend to get lazy in my devotional life." James explained how, with new bursts of enthusiasm and zeal, he determined to pray at a certain time each day. He vowed to read a minimum amount of Scripture. But his good resolves and fine intentions often carried through for only a week. At most a month. Then he would begin slipping and, gradually, he would rouse himself and start trying again.

He paused. He must have read the question marks registering in my expression. "When I say accountable, I know I'm accountable to God. Nothing's more important than that. But I also know that it's important to me to measure up to people I respect. I'd like you to look upon me as a spiritual Christian. Somehow I think that giving account to you of my devotional life would be an incentive to me."

We explored the idea together. At first I tried to think of a diplomatic way of saying that wasn't quite what I had in mind. James realized he was proposing a device. But he also felt it had possibilities. "It's important to me for people to like me . . . to approve of me. In order for people to like me, I feel I have to accomplish. That may be poor Lutheran theology, but it's also where I am in my own life. And in this instance, I'd have to be faithful to you."

James had raised some questions, and it took several days to settle them in my mind. Accountability? Yes, I argued mentally, I believe in that. But when I use the word, I believe in being accountable *to God*. Being accountable to another person was a different matter. At first it sounded as though bones from the ancient cellars of medieval monasticism were creaking out.

And yet it made sense. In the epistle of James, we are exhorted to submit to one another. We've always talked about submission to those in authority over us. And wasn't it also an example of honest caring about each other's spiritual growth? Perhaps it was only the word *accountability* that I objected to. Gradually I discovered myself warming up to James's suggestion.

We decided to make our individual devotional covenants with God. Each decided on a plan of Bible study, a length of time for prayer and reading—even a time of day for study. Then we shared the details with each other. At predetermined times (usually once a week, but we kept that flexible), we agreed to check up on each other. If possible, we'd meet together to share our successes and/or failures as well as to pray together. If our schedules didn't permit a meeting, a few minutes' conversation and prayer by phone would be satisfactory. But, we determined, each time our conversation would focus on our mutual accountability and not be sidetracked into talking about other matters.

I still had slight misgivings, but we tried the experiment. The first week things went marvelously well. I bounded out of bed and began my morning devotions. I had scored that day. All week my record continued.

"James!" I yelled excitedly when we talked on the phone, "I made it! Every morning this week. No failures."

He reported a little difficulty in getting started, but said that after the first few days he, too, was forming a devotional habit.

The second week slipped by as easily as the first. Then came the third week. I should have known that nothing lasts forever.

Wouldn't you know it had to be a Monday morning? Sunday had been a long day—conducting two preaching services, teaching Sunday school, participating in a special program with the young people. Then an emergency pastoral call after the evening worship. Monday morning broke in on me, and I wanted to sneak back under the covers.

"No," I reminded myself, "I have to stick it out." I finished my praying and started with my Bible reading. My eyelids became heavier and heavier. Momentarily I thought ahead of my day. I would have a free period of time from four in the afternoon until nearly seven. I could squeeze in my Bible reading then. I promised myself that I would.

The telephone rang moments after I walked into the house at

4:03. That call tied me up for forty-five minutes. I ran an errand for Shirley I had promised to do nearly a week earlier. Supper was on the table when I returned. Then the whole family left for a special evening meeting.

As I drove along the expressway, it suddenly dawned on me: It's almost nightfall and I haven't done my Bible reading.

Lord, why am I that way? I meant to do it. Then with the call and the errand I simply forgot. And it'll be after 10:30 when we get home. Perhaps even later. Then I'll have to report a failure to James.

With sudden resolution, I prayed, "Father, help me not be too tired when I get home. Please help me stay alert enough to do my Bible reading. If I let up this time, it'll be so much easier to fail next time."

We returned home at 11:15. I did stay up and read. Perhaps that was legalistic, but I felt as if I were being obedient and faithful to God and to James. I'm glad I stayed up.

From that experience I gained some insight into my relationship with James. He himself had said, "I know this is a kind of gimmick." And it was! But it had worked. It had helped me. I believe it also helped James. What we had done, in effect, was to become priests to each other. We had acknowledged our intrinsic unity as Christians.

I've always been an individualistic type of Christian—just Jesus and me. I've not liked accepting the premise that much of my spiritual growth is wrapped up with other believers. Yet the New Testament reminds us over and over that we are, to use the Apostle Paul's analogy, members of a single body. We're exhorted to share in that unity. When we have sickness, we pray for each other. When we experience happiness, we can let it erupt on each other. James's spiritual success means my success as well. When James is stronger as a Christian, the whole body of Christ is strengthened.

James had spoken of himself as a kind of "people pleaser." He did not mean he would hesitate to take a stand on an important issue; he was simply facing honestly the fact that he wanted to be liked, that he sought the approval of others. And he helped me realize that I'm more of a people pleaser than I had wanted to admit.

From the beginning, a sense of mutual caring was built into our relationship. Our growing friendship would not dissipate if either of us failed. But we each knew that the other would feel better about himself and have a deeper self-esteem if he succeeded.

Our relationship continues. We both have successes—and both of us have confessed failures. We can accept each other's failures. But we also remind each other to hang in there! Being accountable to James as well as to God has added an exciting dimension to my life.

Questions for Thought
and Discussion

1. James said, "I need someone to be accountable to." How do you feel about being accountable to another person? Would you have reacted the same way I did?
2. James saw himself as a "people pleaser." Do you often feel that way? Do you feel guilty about it? What's *good* about being a people pleaser?
3. Suppose you decided to set up a relationship such as that described in this chapter. Would having to give an account help you be more faithful?
4. The Bible speaks often of submission to each other. Read Ephesians 5:21-22; Colossians 3:18; James 4:7; 1 Peter 2:13; 1 Peter 5:5. Does the kind of relationship in this chapter seem to fit into the categories these verses refer to?
5. I keep using the word *accountability*. Can you think of another word that might be better? What about *being responsible to?* Would you say that *checking in* would have the same impact?
6. Talk to someone in your group (or a friend if you're doing this individually). Ask him or her to be your prayer partner for one month. Agree to give account of your spiritual faithfulness. At the end of one month, discuss and evaluate the experience.
7. Reflect on the above assignment. Would you be comfortable in giving an account of your spiritual health? If this area isn't easy for you, what areas might you agree to make yourself accountable for? Church attendance? Giving money?
8. What values (including those mentioned in this chapter) can you think of in being accountable to a prayer partner? What disadvantages can you think of?

9. Would it be easy to admit your spiritual failures to another person? Explain your answer.
10. How do you feel about using a "gimmick" to make your prayer life more meaningful?
11. How does James 5: 16 ("Confess your sins to one another.") suggest the idea of accountability?

8
Divine Exchange

AT THE TURN OF THE CENTURY, Charles M. Sheldon wrote a novel which not only reflected liberal theology in its prime, but has greatly influenced generations since. It's called *In His Steps*.

As the story begins, a poor man about thirty years old comes to town. He asks for help, but no one responds. No one except the town minister even gives him a kind word—and the minister might have done more.

One Sunday the poor man stands up in church. The choir has just sung "All for Jesus, All for Jesus." The minister has preached a homiletically acceptable sermon on following in the steps of Jesus.

The beggar challenges the people, saying that a lot of trouble in the world wouldn't exist if people sang the songs like "All for Jesus" and then lived them out. He asks, "But what would Jesus do? Is that what you mean by following in his steps?" Then the man collapses. He is taken to the minister's home, where he dies a few days later.

The next Sunday Rev. Maxwell, the minister, steps into the pulpit of the First Church and faces the people, asking for volunteers to pledge themselves for a period of one year not to do anything without first asking the question, "What would Jesus do?" After asking that question, each will follow Jesus as exactly as he or she knows, no matter what results. A group of people make that commitment, and the rest of the novel details the outcome of that great experiment which ten of those carry out. It revolutionalizes the attitudes of the people involved, and profoundly affects the entire town.

Sounds like an exciting concept, doesn't it? Each time a decision comes up, the person simply asks, "What would Jesus do?" When I first encountered this book, a few months after my conversion, it challenged me. For weeks I tried praying or asking, "What would Jesus do?"

Then one day I came to a startling conclusion: I really couldn't always know the answer to that question. After all, I'm not Jesus! So I did the next best thing. I began praying, "What would Jesus want *me* to do?" Jesus might act quite differently than I. He had a boldness that I sometimes lacked. Jesus faced problems head-on, and sometimes I had to try the retreat-and-wait method. Jesus, because he was sinless, could say, "Repent and leave your sinful ways." Because I am a sinner, I can't command—only urge, "As a fellow sinner, I plead with you to turn to Christ."

When I pray, "What would Jesus want me to do?" it's not really any different from asking, "Lord, what's your will in this situation?"

A few months ago I discovered still another prayer, one which has given me new insight. I call it the divine exchange.

I first heard it during a weekend of lay renewal services. A group of nineteen lay people came to our church from Thursday afternoon through Sunday to conduct worship services, informal home meetings and visit church prospects and delinquent members. At each meeting, at least one of the lay people spoke for a few minutes, sharing some experience from his or her life. One evening a lawyer from Tennessee shared his own experience with the divine exchange prayer. I really don't recall much of what he said that evening, except for the prayer itself. I thought of it often during the weekend. It has since become a significant part of my devotional life.

On a recent Thursday morning I looked at my desk calendar. It was going to be one of those long, demanding days—two committee meetings followed by a counseling appointment. Even lunch was to be a business affair. I felt a sense of weariness come over me.

I love my work as a minister and wouldn't want to do anything else. But it was a kind of day where I felt like crying out, "Lord, give me strength."

That prayer could have been more a cry of exhaustion and frustration than a genuine prayer for God's guidance and strength. But that particular morning, I looked at the two-line prayer which I keep taped on the front of my typewriter.

I sat quietly at my desk and prayed it aloud several times, letting the words sink into my consciousness. In a relaxed spirit I could think about my day's activities again. Peace had now come; I knew my day would be okay. Sure, I would be tired by nine that night, and wouldn't even attempt anything that took a lot of concentration. But I also knew that I was going to have a good day.

The following day I had to make the thirty-minute trip into downtown Atlanta to tape a TV interview. I'd never been on TV before. I'd heard my voice on tape and always felt terribly uncomfortable listening to it. I'm one of those constantly fidgeting people whose jerky movements make him appear to be in a state of constant motion.

"Lord, I'm really nervous about this interview. I'll stutter and say all kinds of dumb things unless you help me."

And then I prayed the divine exchange prayer. The interview went well.

In the past months I've been using that prayer more and more. It's not part of my normal devotional time, but it's a kind of reserve prayer for times when I need peace and assurance that the Lord's working in my life.

The words of this prayer of divine exchange are simple:

> *Lord, today I give you my life;*
> *Now you give me your life.*

Absolutely nothing complicated in that prayer. I've been told that the great nineteenth-century missionary to China, Hudson Taylor, prayed daily these same words or a variation of them. But this simple prayer has a lot of implications for me.

First, *it's a fresh way* for me to say, "I surrender, God." I use it to mean, "My life is yours, Lord." But it's also the other side of the issue. It provides me with an assurance that I'm not merely *giving up* something; I'm also receiving.

This concept plays a large part in my spiritual development. For the first years of my pilgrimage, I lived a negative kind of Christianity. In church I constantly heard what Christians don't do and where we don't go and what we don't say. I'm sure my teachers and pastors said a lot of positive things, but I wasn't hearing.

At times I almost apologized to people for being a Christian. I turned down social invitations from coworkers in the school where I taught. When pressed, I would say, "As a Christian, I can't..." That answer sometimes hurt feelings, and it made me seem smug and out of touch with the rest of the world.

Over the years I've learned to rejoice in the positive side of my Christian experience. I'm no longer intimidated by negatives. I'm free in Jesus Christ. And now that I'm concentrating on the positives, I'm happier. I've discovered a peace that endures. I don't have all the answers to life, but I'm more able to live with its contradictions and paradoxes. People mean more to me. The divine exchange prayer reminds me of this positive aspect of the Christian life.

The divine exchange prayer holds other implications for me. It reminds me of a relationship; it is another way of saying God and I are in this life together. I've not only turned over my life this day to Jesus Christ for him to issue the orders, but I've also said, "Now I expect your love to work in my life today. I want people to recognize that a Holy God is present in my activities."

The best way to explain my feelings about this is to compare it with a story from the fabulous career of Flo Ziegfeld, the great entertainment entrepreneur. Ziegfeld's backers once complained over the exorbitant costs of putting on a musical production. One of them complained, "You have bills here for real silk underwear for the girls. You could buy cheaper. These items aren't seen. Who will know the difference?"

"The girls will know the difference," Ziegfeld replied and closed the matter.

When I keep aware of my relationship with Christ, I know the difference. In those tense moments I find sudden release from tension and anxiety. I may appear no different than I did yesterday or any other time. But I know that Christ is at work directing my life.

Another reason I use the divine exchange prayer is that each time I pray it I make a fresh commitment—it's a way of reaffirming my relationship. Saying to my wife Shirley, "I love you," is another way for me to reaffirm our marriage vows of loving and serving each other with Christ's enablement. And every time I tell her, I strengthen our relationship.

Another reason for this prayer, already implicit above, is the calming effect it has on me. I almost feel like the disciples during the turbulent storm. When they cried out in fear, Jesus awakened. He said simply, "Peace. Stop," and calmness came to the water and to the disciples. That's the kind of effect the divine exchange prayer has for me. When I get harried about the day's activities and pressures, I sometimes need a reminder that I don't have to be frenzied.

It wouldn't have to be this particular prayer. It could as easily be a favorite psalm or a beloved Scripture verse—even a favorite hymn. These have often had the same effect on me, and I appreciate them all. But for me, this divine exchange prayer says it the most clearly and meaningfully. That's why I keep it pasted on the front of my typewriter—a much needed reminder.

And one final reason for praying this prayer—it is a constant reminder that God's involved in my day-to-day activities. Whether I'm preparing a sermon, listening to a troubled friend, waiting for the waitress to bring my lunch, sitting through lengthy committee meetings, or polishing my shoes—the spirit of Jesus Christ is part of that activity.

For instance, suppose I discover that I'm already ten minutes late for an appointment and have to make a left turn onto a busy street. There seems no letup in the traffic, and the seconds tick away. That's a wonderful time for me to remind myself that the Lord's there with me as I wait for a hole in the traffic. He's in control of my life when the toast burns, my ear develops an infection, or an unexpected financial reverse strikes.

Some days I don't pray this prayer—because I don't need it. And it's always great to have those days when the presence of the Lord is terribly real and all's right in my world. But other days come along, the November-afternoon-days, and then I pray:

Lord, today I give you my life;
Now you give me your life.

Questions for Thought
and Discussion

1. Three specific prayers appear in this chapter: (1) What would Jesus do? (2) Lord, what would you have me do? and (3) the divine exchange prayer. Which of the three are you the most comfortable with? The least?

2. In this chapter I explained why I no longer prayed the prayer from *In His Steps*. Can you see where it might be helpful to some people to pray with that question?

3. Silently pray the prayer of divine exchange: "Lord, today I give you my life; now you give me your life." Say this several times. What kind of commitment or exchange are you making?

4. In the chapter I explain why and when I use this prayer. Do you agree? What other times would you find this appropriate?

5. Why is this particular prayer called the divine exchange? Can you think of a better name for it?

6. The words of the divine exchange prayer are not found in the Bible. But there are scriptural passages which contain similar ideas. Read Paul's prayer in Acts 22:10. Does Samson's prayer in Judges 16:28 fall into the category of divine exchange? Can you think of others?

7. Reflect on an incident in which you failed in self-control, in patience, or some other way. How might it have been different had you prayed the divine exchange prayer?

8. Make several copies of the divine exchange prayer. Tape one in a prominent place in your bedroom or perhaps over the bathroom mirror. Make it a place where you'll see it several times a day. Each time you notice the words, pause long enough to read them. Keep another copy in your car.

9

Seven Selfish Prayers

"EACH OF YOU has seven prayers for the rest of your life," said the minister of The Church of the First Humble Order. "Don't waste any of them. They are the only prayers you will have to use on yourselves. Of course, in petitioning God for other people, that number is unlimited. In fact, that's why we're holding you to seven prayers each—so that you can spend your time thinking about other people."

I've invented these words to illustrate a common attitude about prayer. The Church of the First Humble Order has a lot of disciples—in fact, more than I ever dreamed. In just one week, I discovered two members of our local congregation were secret disciples of The Church of the First Humble Order.

First, Elsa. The doctors diagnosed her troubles and said aloud the dreaded word: cancer. She shut herself off from outside visitors, refused to talk about it—even when her husband tried to discuss the subject, she cut him off. One of her friends finally talked to her and asked, "Have you prayed about this?"

"Prayed?" she asked wide-eyed. "Of course not! God's not interested in hearing my prayers for myself."

Elsa's friend opened the Bible to the story of Hezekiah (Isa. 38:1-6). "Look at him—he not only prayed for his own needs, but God answered. Instead of letting him die, God granted the king fifteen additional years."

It took a lot of convincing, but Elsa at least has learned to believe that God grants us the right to pray selfish prayers—even more than seven of them.

The second member of our local congregation is Marc. He's a sincere fellow, and he once said, "God knows my needs. If I started praying about what I needed—well, it seems too selfish. God surely knows anyway. Besides, when I became a Christian I committed my life to him. I said, 'God, you know what's best for me. I put my life into your hands.'"

Marc's words sound very spiritual and noble. And he meant every word. But I also believe he hasn't quite understood the full dimensions of prayer. When we pray, we talk to God about everything that troubles us. I've always had a little rule about what kinds of things to pray for:

Anything big enough for concern is big enough to pray about.

That includes my temper, my driving habits, my financial status, my family relationships, the activities I attend—even the books I read.

If God's concerned about me, I don't think I can be *less* concerned about me. And the Bible makes it very clear just how concerned God is! In the Sermon on the Mount, Jesus said not to worry—God is with us and even our hairs are numbered. He said that God knows when a sparrow falls to the ground. But we're also exhorted in that same sermon to "ask . . . seek . . . knock." The Apostle Paul exhorts us not to worry, but in *everything* by prayer and supplication to make our requests known to God.

I've met a few people who have gone to extremes in this respect. Art and Hazel are examples. For years, when Art would awaken in the morning, he would pray, "Lord, should I wear the blue tie with the red design or the red tie with the blue checks?" Then he'd pray, "Father, should I catch the 7:35 bus or the 8:02?" Hazel confesses that she often prayed, "God, how long should I bake the turkey?" Or, "Would it be all right if I washed dishes now and then vacuumed? Or should I vacuum first?"

While Art and Hazel may have been going a bit too far, I applaud their intentions. They wanted every area of their lives subjected to God's will. They tried to be careful to hear his direction in every action.

Art and Hazel have changed a lot since I first met them, and now they can even laugh at some of their actions. "We had a lot to learn and we're still learning," Art said one day recently. "Some of the things we did sound stupid, but we'd rather pray about a lot of little things we can handle ourselves than to miss praying over important matters. And, I don't know a verse in the Bible that says to stop praying, do you?"

Most people don't go to the extremes of Hazel and Art. A lot of them are like a woman I met about a year ago, when Shirley and I attended a dinner for local writers in Atlanta. This woman introduced herself to me as soon-to-be-published author of a gothic novel. I told her I wrote religious/inspirational books and she, naturally, asked their titles. When I mentioned one on prayer, she smiled and leaned back. "Yes, prayer. But people really bother God about so many petty things, don't they? God has enough to do without being concerned over my insignificant problems all the time." She paused long enough to smile indulgently, and then asked, "Don't you agree?"

Shirley spoke up before I had a chance and said, "If that's the case, why does God say to pray without ceasing? Or why do we find so many verses in the Bible telling us to pray about things?"

The lady smiled magnanimously and then, as if talking to a none-too-bright child, said, "About big things, of course. But certainly not my problems—you know, the everyday ones. God's got bigger things to do than that." I don't remember the rest of the discussion, but I got her message: Don't bother God with earthbound problems.

Other people have expressed the same idea. I sat in on an adult Sunday school class one morning. The subject of prayer had come up. Gary said, "I feel God's got so many other things more important than me. It's almost as if I wanted to glue him into my world so that he spent all his time taking care of just me."

"Isn't God big enough to do that for everybody?" Suzie's timid voice asked.

The discussion went on for quite awhile. Then Suzie, in her customary honesty said, "I wonder if those are the real reasons for not praying. One reason I don't pray more about myself and for my needs is that it puts faith right on the line. It means I've got to commit myself to ask God and also be prepared to receive his answers. And then sometimes I ask myself, 'But what if God doesn't answer?' So in my case, it's simply a lack of faith."

Several heads nodded. Likely, people have different reasons for not praying for their own needs. Yet all the time the Bible declares: "You do not have because you do not ask" (James 4:2). The key phrase of Philippians 4:6–7 is "in everything [give thanks]." That means in every circumstance or situation. The Living Bible paraphrases this passage as: "Don't worry about anything; instead, pray about everything; tell God your needs."

It disturbs me that members of the Church of the First Humble Order are now infiltrating congregations. They work with subtle methods, often entrapping folks before they realize what's happening to them.

These incipient revolutionists pound away at certain concepts such as *selfishness*. "If we really care about people, we put them before our own needs," a spokesperson for the First Humble Order declares. "It's simple: Jesus first, others second, and ourselves last. Take the first letter of those three words and you have J-O-Y, and joy is what we find. Reverse the order and you don't have joy." Doesn't that sound spiritual? I don't know any scriptural basis, but it has a kind of holy ring about it!

I find this principle working in some of the strangest places. For instance, one day I sat in a different adult Sunday school class. Near the end of the period together, the teacher said several things that gave me new insight into a situation with which I had been grappling. As soon as the class was over I said, "Harold, thanks for what you said." I explained how helpful it had been.

"Just thank the Lord," he said with a smile on his face. "He's the one who did it."

With some people that might have sounded like phony piety,

but not with Harold. I knew he was sincere. "But brother," I said, "of course the Holy Spirit made the truth a reality to you. He used you to deliver it."

He said, "But I want to hide myself behind the cross, so that people see only Jesus Christ. No glory for me."

I couldn't make Harold understand what I wanted to say. God had given the man teaching gifts and used him. It's not selfish to recognize one's gifts or to use them for the uplifting of other people.

The Church of the First Humble Order also uses another ploy, very close to this one—the idea of *worthlessness*. "I'm nothing; Jesus is everything." That really sounds humble. But God doesn't seem to speak that way. He called Paul a chosen vessel, David the apple of his eye, Abraham his friend. In Romans 16, the Apostle Paul holds up accolades for faithful coworkers in the Lord.

We're not worthless; we're special just because we're human. And we don't have to save our seven prayers for ourselves, to be used sparingly. Rather than counting ourselves as nothing, each of us can say, "By his grace, I am something." The chief Apostle said, "By the grace of God I am what I am" (1 Cor. 15:10).

I'm determined to stamp out the Church of the First Humble Order. It takes effort and vigilance, but it can be done! Two things I've found helpful in reminding myself how to combat this attitude:

First, *our own needs are the natural place to begin praying.* And God begins his work with the most obvious needs—he starts where we hurt. Could I honestly be concerned about twenty other sick people if my pain keeps reminding me of my own sickness? Could I pray effectively for fifteen troubled marriages until I've prayed about the weaknesses in my own? When I'm without a job, isn't my need more pressing to me than praying for John to get a pay increase?

Think of the biblical accounts of people Jesus met. They cried out to him with their most obvious needs—"Son of David, have mercy on me." Or, "That I might receive my sight." And he began his ministry to them from that point. Second Chronicles contains a beautiful prayer in which Solomon, about to become king, asks God to grant him wisdom. And this request became the basis for a long and fruitful reign.

Second, *answering "selfish" prayers gives God pleasure.* The Bible declares that God delights in his people, that he loved the world and sent Jesus. So to ask for specific needs in our lives is, to me, like asking a loving parent to be concerned about the needs of his or her child.

I'm putting the members of the Church of the First Humble Order on notice. I'm out to defeat you. God gives me unlimited resources to talk to him about my needs. As I walk more obediently, the Spirit will teach me to pray more effectively for myself and for others.

So, First Humble Order—beware!

Questions for Thought
and Discussion

1. Some Christians feel it is selfish to pray for their own needs. What's the difference between selfish and self-centered, between self-loving and self-caring?
2. Read again my simple rule for prayer, on page 78. Can you give a better rule or improve on it?
3. If God cares about our needs, do you agree it's all right for us to be concerned as well?
4. As you read about Art and Hazel, what kind of inner reaction did you have? Too fanatic? Too simple-minded? Or did you sense they were people seeking a more committed prayer life?
5. The novelist I met differentiated between "big problems" and "my problems, the everyday ones." Does God, as she asserted, "have bigger things to do" than answering my needs? If he's God, can't he handle all the needs—both small and great?
6. How do you feel about Suzie's answer to Gary? Would you agree? Can you think of other reasons people hesitate to ask God for their own needs?
7. Read Philippians 4:6-7 in at least two different translations. What do you think the Apostle Paul means? How does this apply to praying for your own needs?
8. How do you feel when you present your own needs to God? Selfish? Worthless? Confident? Hesitant?
9. Visualize yourself standing along the Jericho road. Jesus is passing through on his way to Jerusalem. He approaches, stands in front of you and says, "What do you want from me?" What will you answer?
10. In order to help me stamp out the Movement of the Church of the First Humble Order, please stop right now, and silently make eight specific requests expressing *your* need.

10

The Sign of
the Wool

Max felt caught. He would enjoy coaching Little League. But
he also enjoyed Thursday bowling with Ralph and others from
his office. And they bowled all summer long.

Max prayed about the matter for several days. He seemed no
closer to the answer than when he had started. "Lord, if you
want me to coach Little League, then . . . uh, then have Melvin
call me before noon today and ask if I've made up my mind."

Within an hour the telephone rang and Melvin asked, "Have
you made up your mind yet?"

"Uh, not yet, but I'll let you know soon," Max replied.

He prayed again. "Lord, how about two out of three?"

It's rather evident what Max wanted. Asking God for a sign
was really an attempt to manipulate God into confirming Max's
own preference.

Yet there are times when I believe it is perfectly honest and acceptable for a Christian to ask God for a sign. We have biblical
evidence for this.

Tucked into the middle of the book of Judges is the story of
Gideon. Not a prominent man. Nothing about him suggested
greatness. But one day God said, "Okay, Gideon, you're the one!
Lead my people against the Midianites and defeat them!"

What a staggering thought! A poor farm boy called by God.

The complete story is found in Judges 6. Gideon replied to
God, "If now I have found favor with thee, then show me a sign
that it is thou who speakest with me" (6:17).

God answered Gideon, who then made his first counterattack against the Midianites. He ran into opposition. Battle lines were drawn, and Gideon sent word to able-bodied men of Israel to fight.

Then Gideon had second thoughts. Has God really called *me?* He prayed for guidance again, wanting assurance he was doing the right thing. Gideon said, "I am laying a fleece of wool on the threshing floor; if there is dew on the fleece alone, and it is dry on all the ground, then I shall know that thou wilt deliver Israel by my hand, as thou hast said" (6:37).

Judges 6:38 says succinctly, "And it was so. When he rose early next morning and squeezed the fleece, he wrung enough dew from the fleece to fill a bowl with water."

Enough for Gideon? Not quite. He said, "Don't get angry, God, but let's try it the other way. Let only the fleece be dry and the ground around be wet."

"And God did so that night; for it was dry on the fleece only, and on all the ground there was dew" (6:4).

Gideon never doubted the call again. He went on to great victory after that incident. And from the story of Gideon we have what we in religious circles often call "putting out a fleece." This term means asking for a sign. For proof. For assurance. For guidance.

Max asked, but I believe he already knew what God wanted. God answered anyway. The implication is strong that Gideon, too, already knew, but lacked the courage to step out. (Would you suddenly stand up and announce to the world that God had called you to rid the world of all atheists?)

In Exodus 3:4, we read that God called Moses to deliver the people of Israel. The patriarch hesitated, either from sincere doubt of God's call or perhaps from the immensity of the task. Twice God said he'd give Moses a sign.

In the New Testament, God spoke to Peter in a dream or vision. He used that as a means to tell Peter that the gospel must not be limited to Jews but proclaimed to all people, for "God is no respecter of persons." There is no record that Peter specifically asked for a sign. Jesus had said, as part of his final message to the disciples, "You shall be my witnesses ... to the end of the earth" (Acts 1: 8). Now God was making it clear to Peter that the sharing with Gentiles is what he required. He provided a sign to a disciple who either hadn't grasped God's will or was reluctant to obey.

God speaks through the "putting out of the fleece" when he wishes to lead us in a certain direction—and we're reluctant to go that way. Both Gideon and Peter knew, or had strong reason to know, God's will. They shrank back. Perhaps they struggled with the immensity of the command. But they were also disciples who were willing to be convinced.

There are times when not only is it proper to put out a fleece, but when to do so actually honors God:

First, *when there is genuine doubt*. And doubts come on many levels. Not doubt of God's existence or presence in our lives, but doubt regarding a specific task or course of action. All of Peter's background and Jewish training argued against his suddenly ministering to Gentiles. No wonder he doubted.

During the summer of 1974 I put out a fleece. I was working in a nonpastoral position which I knew was temporary. Several churches contacted me, and one in Alabama sounded attractive. Shirley and I visited that church after their pulpit committee heard me preach. We met the committee, talked openly with them several hours. Later Shirley commented, "I think we could be happy here."

I thought so, too. Yet there was the lack of certainty. I could not feel a definite conviction of yes or no. Everything seemed fine. Opportunities presented themselves. Challenges loomed before us. The church appeared open to new suggestions.

"I'll give you a definite answer in two weeks," I promised as we left the people. Two weeks would make it Wednesday, June 12, 1974. I said I would call before noon.

Each day we prayed, but nothing became clearer. I told the Lord, "If you don't intervene by June 12, I intend to answer yes."

On Sunday, June 9, I preached at a small church in suburban

Atlanta while the pastor was in the hospital. A pulpit committee came, but that was nothing unusual. And knowing the nature of most pulpit committees, I expected weeks to pass before I heard anything. I prayed, "Lord, if this new pulpit committee represents where you want us to go, I remind you that Wednesday morning is your deadline."

That Sunday afternoon at 2:30 the phone rang. The caller gave his name, then said, "I'm on the pulpit committee that heard you this morning. We'd like to meet with you."

"Okay," I replied, beginning to wonder if the Lord was sending in a message to us. "When?"

"Monday night all right with you?"

"Sure," I replied in amazement.

Afterwards I prayed, "Lord, this is hard to believe. But there's still the deadline. It's getting closer." Even after talking with a prospective pastor, pulpit committees often take weeks to finalize agreements. It was up to the Lord now.

We met with the pulpit committee nearly two hours. Everything felt right, and yet several times I wondered about the deadline. Finally the chairman looked around and said to the others, "Any more questions?" No one spoke. "Well, Mr. Murphey, would you accept a call to become our pastor?"

"I certainly will." And I knew it was right. God had answered my fleece with only slightly more than twenty-four hours to spare!

That's one valid reason for using a fleece—you honestly don't know God's will but want to know. It's another way of saying, "Lord, I commit myself to your will. But I need to know what you want of me so I can do it."

A second reason for using a fleece: *assurance.* Who is so filled with faith that he or she can always say, "I know God's will"? Or even proclaim, "No matter what God wants, I'll do it without hesitation or reservation"? This matter of the fleece can often be the extra nudge needed to make the decision.

I've heard people speak against the fleece, claiming it nullifies the element of faith. I believe that, on the contrary, putting out a fleece is actually a sign of faith. It's like saying, "God, I believe you will show me the way. I'm waiting for you to give an answer through some external means." That often takes deep faith to say.

Mona told me about an incident in her life using the fleece. She felt God wanted her to enter into Christian work. She was a well-educated, middle-aged housewife who could give all kinds of rational explanations why God couldn't possibly want *her* to do such a thing. One morning she was working in her kitchen. For nearly a week Mona had been looking for the lid to a particular jar. She had searched the drawer, and in fact the whole kitchen, several times without success. "Okay, Father, I'm giving up. If you help me find that jar lid—right now—not only will I thank you, but I'll also accept that as a final word about my future."

Mona opened the drawer and suddenly saw the lid. Had it been there all along? She didn't ask. She thanked God. And while I found myself cringing a little inside upon hearing that true story (after all, I thought, I would never have asked God to use a jar lid!), Mona never doubted. She carries that lid around inside her purse. Sometimes she fingers it, reminding herself of God's call.

A jar lid. A fleece. A date on the calendar. Does the object matter? Isn't it rather just another way of praying for God's guidance?

Questions for Thought and Discussion

1. On page 85 I use the phrase "an attempt to manipulate God." What kind of feelings does that stir up in you? How do you sometimes attempt to manipulate God's will in your prayer?
2. Compare Max and Gideon. With which of the two do you identify?
3. Recall an experience in which you asked God for a sign. Did you get one? Did you feel reluctant to ask for a sign? Is this a principle method you have for receiving guidance?
4. Recall an incident when you prayed for guidance, yet in your heart you already knew what God wanted. What kind of feelings did you have? How did you finally resolve the matter?
5. Recall an incident when you weren't sure of God's will. You put out a fleece and it came out positive. Or one in which it came out negative. Describe the experience.
6. In the Bible God gave other signs to his people. Read and explain
   (a) Genesis 9: 11–17
   (b) Isaiah 7: 10–14
   (c) Luke 2: 12
   (d) Would you consider Acts 10: 9–29 a sign also?
   Can you think of other biblical events in which God gives a sign?
7. On page 87, one reason listed for putting out a fleece is genuine doubt. I wrote the incident about accepting a call to a church in Alabama. Would you have put out a fleece? Why or why not? What other method could I have used along with or instead of putting out a fleece?
8. How can putting out a fleece be merely a copout, so that you don't have to accept the responsibility for your own de-

90

cision? Have you ever used it that way? Or known of someone who has?

9. The second reason I give for putting out a fleece (p. 88) is
for assurance. What's the difference between genuine doubt
and the need for assurance? Do you think it honors God
when you ask for an "extra nudge"? Give a reason for your
answer.

10. I contend that putting out a fleece doesn't nullify faith (pp.
88–89), but honors God. Can you see how people might
disagree with me? How do you feel about putting out a
fleece?

11. Read again the story about Mona and the jar lid. Would
you have used an experience like that for determining the
divine will? What dangers can you see?

12. You have become dissatisfied with your present job and
have started praying about a different one. You put out a
fleece: if a new job is *offered,* you will accept it. The next
day, you receive an unsolicited job offer from another company. How would you handle this? Would you, without
qualification, accept this as the will of God? Continue praying? Ask for a second sign?

11

Let's Make a Contract!

"PRAY FOR ME. I'm going through a difficult time," Alice whispered as she brushed past me at the church door.

I wanted to pray for her needs—and I did. But how long did she expect me to pray? Every day for a week? A full month? Forever?

Her request reminded me of a problem my wife encountered. She had been ten years old when Floyd and Hank conducted evangelistic meetings in her home church. She had sat fascinated as they dramatized the gospel for children.

On the final evening, the evangelists had said, "We need your prayers. How many of you will promise to pray for us every day?"

Dozens of hands went up. Shirley's was among them.

The next day Floyd and Hank left. Shirley never saw them again. For years she prayed every day for them—after all, she had promised. Shirley was nearly twenty-one before she stopped. Their faces had long been pushed into the back of her memory; she could scarcely recall either their messages or their personalities. She knew only that she had promised to pray every day for them.

"I finally stopped," she says, "and for a long time afterward a sense of guilt would come over me. I realized that probably few—if any—of the others who had promised to pray were still keeping at it. But I had made a promise. I wasn't sure how long I ought to keep praying."

I'm not sure either. Yet this kind of request comes to me often.
How long should I pray? Sometimes the time element is easy.
On June 25, Suzanne called. "I'm going to speak to a group
called Parents Without Partners. This is not a religious group as
such, but I've been invited to tell them how, as a Christian without a husband, I raised three children. The meeting will be July
21. Please pray as I prepare so that I'll only speak what the Lord
wants me to say."

Her request was simple. I prayed every day from June 25
through July 21. Then my petitions on that issue were over. But
other times—and, in fact, most times—the matter is not quite so
clear.

Frequently people impulsively blurt out, "Pray for me." Sometimes it may be only a space filler; sometimes it may be a plea
which means, "I just need your attention and love." Or it may
mean, "Oh, I wish someone would pray earnestly for me."

Recently I asked friends how they handled these requests. One
said, "Frankly, I forget most of them. I show interest at that time.
I think that's all they really want."

Another who admitted not following through said, "I seldom
promise to pray, and if I don't make a promise, then I can't be
held guilty for not praying, can I?"

Another answered, "I pray when people ask. I pray then and
there on the spot. And I tell them, 'As often as I think about you
in the days ahead, I'll pray for this request again.' "

The first two answers seemed completely contrary to the way
I felt about honoring the requests of others. I tried the latter.
But I soon discovered a problem. It was easy enough to pray for
a need for a few days. But other seemingly more pressing matters
crowded out yesterday's problems. Last week's priorities became
forgotten history as I plunged into new activities. Then, perhaps
weeks later, pangs of guilt would stab at me. *I had forgotten!*

It was made worse when, weeks afterwards, a friend would
again refer to one of those requests. The conversation often
made me uncomfortable: "Remember when I asked you to pray
for my brother to quit his heavy drinking? He hasn't had a
drink in nearly three weeks. He's even holding down a steady

job and goes to church with his family. Thanks for praying for me."

I can always rejoice in the good news. But I can also feel hypocritical for letting that person assume I had been faithfully praying when I had totally forgotten.

About six months ago I hit upon an idea which has helped me in listening and responding to specific prayer requests. I call it *contract praying*.

Contract praying works like this: Recently Earl brought his nephew Larry into my office. Larry had been in the mental health clinic for almost three months. He had now been discharged and was significantly better. However, he still faced periodic depression. We prayed for Larry that night. "I feel so much better," he said as he left. "Please keep praying for me."

Rather than simply promising to pray, I said, "First, Larry, tell me specifically what you want me to pray for. Your general mental attitude? Your ability to work? I find it easier to pray when I ask God for specific things."

He hesitated only a second before replying, "Ask God to rid me of these deep moods of depression. I know I can make it if I don't fall into that again."

"Okay, Larry," I said. "Here's what I'll do. For the next month I intend to pray for you every single day. At the end of that time I will stop unless I hear from you to continue. If you contact me and ask me to keep on or to pray differently, then I'll make another agreement with you."

"Hey, I never heard anything about praying like that before," he said, and his face brightened. "And—and you'll be praying *every* day?"

I nodded.

I carry an appointment book in my shirt pocket. I have a taped-in sheet with my daily prayer requests. At the top I have typed in requests that have no time factor—my family, my own spiritual growth, various friends, missionaries, groups about which I'm concerned. The bottom half of the page contains several names written in pencil with dates after them.

For instance, at this moment I have, among others, the follow-

ing penciled items: Suzie C. 8/4; Ken 9/1; Retreat 7/8–9. Trans-
lated, these entries mean: Pray for Suzie C., who is having a real
battle with her faith. The original agreement was for one
month; this has been renegotiated for another month. Ken is a
man who left the ministry two years ago because of deep personal problems. He is now on top again, and moving toward
the pastorate. By September 1, he ought to be settled; I promised
to talk to my Father about him every day until then. On July 8
and 9, our church has an officers' retreat, and I have specific requests for that event.

I see at least three benefits from contract praying. First, *I think
it means a lot to people to know not only that you pray for them,
but that you pray specifically and daily.* They realize you are
responding to their need with concern. You also leave the door
open for them to talk about the situation again. How much
better a way is there to show a person you really care about what
happens in his or her life?

Second, *the penciled notes remind me to pray.* Martin's need
for a job may be uppermost in my thoughts today. But after visiting four people in the hospital, getting involved in an elder's
domestic squabble, preparing sermons and Sunday school lessons, Martin's problems are apt to slip out of my conscious thinking. My note helps me remember.

Third, *a time limit frees me.* I make a promise, and when the
time expires I either renegotiate or stop altogether. This prevents
a great deal of guilt from creeping in.

Two years ago, one of my professors became president of his
college. At the alumni luncheon, the president of the alumni association said, "We want to pledge our support to our new president. Those who will promise to pray every day for him, please
stand!" Everyone in the room stood.

I can't begin to judge their faithfulness—and that's not my
business anyway. But I have his name typed in on my prayer list.
I suppose that as long as he is president I shall remember him
every day. But all requests I receive aren't the kind I want to

pray for perpetually. That is when I find contract praying helpful.

The next time a friend asks you to pray, why don't you say, "Sure! Let's make a prayer contract!" You may find it makes your prayer life more effective.

Questions for Thought and Discussion

1. When someone says, "Pray for me," do you feel honored? Imposed upon? Take them seriously? Treat it as a habitual phrase instead of a request?
2. Do you admire Shirley's faithfulness? Laugh at her childlike persistence? Would you have continued praying for that many years?
3. Shirley felt guilty for stopping, even after several years. Have you ever experienced guilt over not praying when you promised you would? If so, how did you handle or get rid of your sense of guilt?
4. Recall an incident when you made any kind of promise and didn't keep it. How did you justify or excuse yourself?
5. Can you think of a situation when you might
   (a) put someone in a bind with your request, as the evangelists did Shirley?
   (b) make a commitment and either regret it or fail to fulfill it?
6. How do you react when you get a request like the one from Suzanne? What makes you think she really means it?
7. Would you feel free enough to contact three people with a request like Suzanne's? Explain how you'd feel about asking other people.
8. Recall an experience in which you prayed for a specific need over a definite period of time and saw the results. Describe the events and especially your feelings.
9. Recall an experience in which you were asked to pray over a period of time, but the person never mentioned the request again. How did you feel? Indifferent? As though the other person didn't really care? Miffed? Angry?
10. Compare the requests of the evangelists with that of

Suzanne. How could they have better handled their request?

11. You are facing major surgery in sixteen days. You decide to ask three friends to make a prayer contract with you. Exactly what will you ask?

12. You have been asked to pray for a specific need from June 21 through July 21. How often would you pray? On June 27 you realize you have forgotten to pray two days in a row. How would you feel about forgetting?

13. Someone says to you (cf. p. 94), "Remember when I asked you to pray for my sister's husband?" You either forgot or neglected to pray. How do you respond to that question?

14. I listed 3 benefits of contract praying (p. 94). Do you see these as benefits? Can you think of others? How would you feel if you knew that at least one other person prays for you every day?

15. Think of one need you have. Be as specific as you can—nothing general such as "Pray that I'll be a stronger Christian." Ask one person in your group (or, if you are using this book individually, contact one friend) to pray for this need. Be sure to include the time element of one month. At the end of the month, contact your prayer partner for a report.

12

"Okay, Lord, I Give Up"

I WANTED TO write the book.

The whole process started with a casual question. An editor, aware of my writing, verbalized the need for a book about women in the church. He had seen several books, but all of them appeared either too narrow or far too broad. "Why don't you try your hand?" he asked.

That question sparked my interest. I mulled it over for several days and my friend and I talked two or three times.

He even had a publisher lined up. I forged ahead in research. For me, research meant not only talking to people but reading all the pertinent literature available. It also entailed intensively studying several key biblical passages.

Soon I had three chapters and an outline completed. I was on my way.

Then the trouble began. I can't explain the feeling, only a sense that the pieces simply didn't fit together.

But why? Had I taken a wrong theological position? Was I too narrow myself? Was I too far out in my thinking?

Then I prayed, "Lord, help me. I really want to do this book. Give your guidance." I expected to find that the writing went easier, but it didn't. The paragraphs didn't come out right. I couldn't seem to express my ideas freely.

For the next several days I prayed more fervently than ever. "Maybe I've hit writer's block." Praying became even more fervent.

Three days later I said to Shirley, "Please pray with me about this book. It isn't moving well. I need help."

"I'll pray," she said, "but I'm prejudiced. I didn't think you ought to do the book in the first place."

"Why didn't you tell me? I mean, I would have prayed a lot more about it before I tackled it."

"You didn't ask me. You just started in. Remember?"

Right, of course. It's happened several times in my life; I've jumped into a project with much enthusiasm and little guidance. I suppose I've often mistaken one for the other. This subject had really intrigued me; it was timely and relevant.

"But ... but ..." I sputtered, "look at the hours of research I've done. The three completed chapters, the detailed outline ..."

"Okay," she said softly. "I'll pray with you. I only wanted you to know that I'm not praying with a completely open mind."

We prayed together. I *did* say, "Lord, if it's not what you want me to do, then show me. Take away the desire on my part. But ..." And I went into several sentences telling God how significant I felt the book was.

No answer. No feeling. No indications.

Two days later I was walking from the parking lot to a local hospital on my way to visit a patient. I prayed, half-aloud, "Lord, I need some direction. Please guide me. I'll give this up if that's what you want ..."

I stopped praying in the middle of the sentence. I knew the answer: *Give it up.*

"But Father ..." I began to argue. "The hours of reading and background and ..." But the Lord had spoken to me. I had that inner certainty of his will.

"Okay, I give it up."

And peace descended on a struggling soul. I relinquished the book.

I've had to pray prayers of relinquishment several times in my life. And I've discovered that it doesn't always mean the same thing! In this case it meant loss for me. Or at least it meant giving up something dear to myself.

Most Christians have struggled over letting go or giving up things which hinder our relationship to Christ. One man I know raised show dogs. He became far too attached to them and felt that they interfered with his commitment to his family and the Lord. "I kept telling God how I could witness for him . . . and how I always went to Sunday worship. But God wanted me, and he wanted the best of me. I knew that my hobby had come before God in my life." Then he added, "Once in awhile I miss my dogs—but I know that I couldn't commit myself wholeheartedly to both."

However, relinquishment isn't always loss. Abraham knew that—because he experienced the lesson.

Think of how the patriarch must have felt. After years of childlessness, God told him he would have a son. And Abraham was seventy-five then. He waited a full twenty-five years before the event took place. And can't you imagine how he must have loved that son! One day he discovered how much he really loved Isaac. God said, "Abraham, take your son Isaac, and go to Mount Moriah. Take him and offer him as a sacrifice."

Abraham went out to do exactly as his God had commanded. What faith! What commitment! And how the old man must have wept inwardly. But the biblical writer doesn't tell us of any struggle going on with Abraham. It simply states that he obeyed. He took the boy to the mountain and tied the lad down, got the fire ready to light—even raised his hand to stab his son. And what happened?

"Stop!" cried out the voice of God.

The Bible says God was testing Abraham. That's sometimes how we need to see relinquishment. What does a person, a job, a hobby, a career mean to us? When it becomes a matter of "my wife or my God," what's the choice? I suspect that the real lesson in the story of Abraham is not that God wanted to take away Abraham's son, but that God wanted to take away the father's preoccupation with his son.

Perhaps it's like the question Jesus asked Peter after the resurrection. "Do you love me more than these?" (John 21:15). Let the theologians argue over whether Jesus was referring to the actual fish or the occupation of fishing. I'm content to think that Jesus asked the supreme question: "Are you more attached to me than you are to anything else?"

A third concept is involved in the matter of relinquishment—merely putting something aside as a temporary measure. I wonder about Moses' relinquishment. He knew God had called him to deliver the Jews out of Egyptian slavery. He even tried to stop a fight between a Hebrew slave and an Egyptian. He ended up murdering the Egyptian and had to flee from the land.

He spent forty years taking care of sheep. Moses must have thought and rethought his calling a long time while he walked with the sheep and slept under the stars. Had Yahweh really called him?

Somewhere along the way, he must have given up his claim. He relinquished his divine destiny and became a shepherd. Then the Lord of heaven appeared in a burning bush and commanded, "Set my people free."

Moses may have relinquished his real calling—but only for a time.

When Shirley and I first felt the call to Africa, we wrote to mission boards. We contacted missionaries. We even began saving to help pay our own fare to Africa. Yet every action we took seemed to lock the door tighter.

One morning I said, "Okay, Lord, I felt you wanted us in Africa. Either I was mistaken or something else is wrong. I give up. I'm not going to make any plans toward going until you take the first step!"

For the next two or three years God directed our lives in a variety of ways. But when we prayed about Africa, the answer was silence. Then, long after we had put aside any plans or hopes, God spoke to us again.

"Honey," Shirley said, "I believe it's time to make plans for Africa." It was the Lord's timing. Now we waited for him. We had relinquished our claim to Africa. We didn't lose it, or give it up—although it may have seemed that way at first. But we did put it aside.

There's another phase of relinquishment: giving up the good in order to get something better.

Jim received a tempting job offer. There was only one hitch; it meant relocating. "I don't even mind that, except I feel close to the people in this church. This church has become my family," the forty-year-old bachelor said. "I've not found any place like this before."

He wrestled with the job for a few days, and then headed from Atlanta toward the Pacific Northwest. He got halfway there, and then called us. "I'm coming back. I've prayed about it. I've decided to take a lesser job rather than to leave all of you."

He returned, and no job opened for him immediately. In fact, he existed through the help of Christian friends, unemployment benefits and a few odd jobs he picked up from time to time. Then one day he found a wonderful job. "My, this was worth waiting for," he said.

I asked him, "Jim, did you ever feel you had made a mistake in not going west?" He smiled and shook his head. "*I* wanted to go west, but when I prayed I knew I belonged here. I also knew God had something better for me. Even though it took a little time, it's been worth the wait."

This all comes under the idea of relinquishment—it's a way of testing for ourselves where our loyalties really lie. We hold on to the most precious things in life, even though we're willing to give up those of lesser value.

In the Bible, Job suffered and lost every material possession. Then the members of his own family died. Finally he lost his own health. But one thing Job didn't lose—his trust in the God of heaven. He held on, refusing to relinquish his faith. And God blessed him for his stance.

Are you holding on to something you need to let go? This loving God may withhold the *good* from you, but only so he can give you the best!

Questions for Thought
and Discussion

1. Can you identify with me in my frustration over the writing project? How would it feel to get immersed in an activity and then discover that wasn't what God wanted you to do?
2. Can you recall an incident in your life similar to this? What did you do? Did you finish carrying out the activity? Quit in the middle? If you're with a group, share some of your feelings before and after you made your decision.
3. In this chapter I give several reasons we sometimes need to relinquish what is important to us. Look back over the chapter and point out the ones you notice.
4. Think of yourself as Abraham, after God has asked him to sacrifice his son. (You may want to read Genesis 22.) We're only told the facts of the story. Go through that story and try to imagine the feelings of Abraham.
4. Now compare yourself with Abraham. Although God probably wouldn't ask you to kill the person nearest you, suppose God asked you to give that one up through accidental death. How would you feel?
5. Suppose Jesus walked into your life. Instead of seeing fish and boats as he did with Peter, he would see you surrounded by the things you love and treasure. Now he asks, "Do you love me more than these?" How would you answer?
6. Can you think of others in the Bible God tested for their loyalty? What about Hezekiah? Job?
7. Why does God test us? (see Genesis 22:1). After all, doesn't he know everything in our hearts?
8. Can you think of an experience in your life when you've settled for the good and missed out on the best? Can you think of an experience when you were ready to settle for the good, but the Lord turned you around to receive the best?

If you're in a group, briefly share one or the other of these experiences.

9. Can you make a distinction between our *relinquishment* and God's *testing?* How can they also be connected or similar?

13

Responding to the Need

MEL POKED ME and then motioned with his head as he whispered, "There goes Greg again." And there he was—tall, wafer-thin, and moving toward the front of the church. He knelt down, and soon two or three others joined him.

Because I attended a Christian college, we had chapel every day. And frequently missionaries spoke at our chapel services. They quoted liberally from the words of Jesus: "The fields are already white for harvest" (John 4:35). "The harvest is plentiful, but the laborers are few; pray therefore the Lord of the harvest to send out laborers into his harvest" (Matt. 9:37-38).

We opened our hymnals to songs such as "Where He Leads Me I Will Follow" or the one that says, "Lord of harvest, send forth reapers..." Or perhaps even, "Oh send me, send me forth I pray."

Then most of them concluded their messages with a plea for workers in the harvest fields of the world. And Greg always went forward. As I got to know Greg better I realized he wasn't just the perpetual guy who signed up for everything. He went because, as he said, "I was responding to a need. I want always to keep saying, 'God, I'm available. So use me if you want!'"

It was not only the call for foreign missions. When any need was presented in our chapels, Greg always responded. He made himself available to the Lord to be a minister, answering any challenge that came along. When one speaker told of his work with impoverished whites in Appalachia, Greg took an extra job

for one semester so that he could help those less fortunate than
he.

In responding to the needs around him, Greg was following
the example of the boy Samuel, who responded to the call of
God with the words, "Speak Lord, for thy servant hears" (1 Sam.
3:10). And God wants us to listen to the needs around us and
make ourselves available.

But I wonder if many times we're not guilty of responding to a
need when we need to respond to God's *will*. Sometimes we get
pressured and manipulated into jobs and activities that God
hasn't asked us to do. We get too taken up with responding to
needs and don't know how to limit our response to the will of
God. And the difference can cause us a lot of trouble.

It certainly caused Moses trouble. He responded to the cries
of help from his oppressed race. They were in bondage, held
down by their Egyptian captors. When he saw an Egyptian
badly treating an Israelite, Moses intervened. In the process, he
killed the Egyptian.

God wasn't telling Moses to kill the man. Moses responded
to a need. As a result he had to flee Egypt. Forty years later, God
called him to deliver the nation from its enemies. Then Moses
was hearing the voice of the Lord, not just responding to a need.

One of my struggles is knowing which needs to respond to.
And part of realizing my limitations is acknowledging that I
can't possibly respond to all the hands that reach toward me. I
have to make choices.

The process of making choices is where we learn to hear what
God wants us to do and not merely respond to pressure, guilt, or
emotion. Here's an experience still fresh in my thinking. Near
my home there are two colleges where I have taught one or two
courses at a time. I stopped teaching at both because of the sheer
limitation of my time and my energy. Recently the head of one
of the colleges contacted me. "How about teaching again? I've
got a course you'd really love—just made for you."

"I don't think so," I responded. "My church and my writing
are about all I can do right now."

"This one is a course you could do so well . . ." and he explained, mentioning how much he had appreciated my work in the past and how positively the students had responded to my teaching.

"All I can do is pray about it," I answered. "My inclination is to say no, but I'll ask the Lord about it."

I prayed all week for guidance. In my heart I had mixed feelings. They needed a good teacher, and their faculty was already overworked. I could ease the situation. And I love teaching. After a week it became apparent to me that God was saying no. And I declined the position. Had I agreed to teach, it would have been either because of my concern for the college or my own internal pressure to respond to a need that I felt I could meet.

Life's always going to present the Christian with those kinds of choices. And those choices hit us in the church as much as anywhere else: "As I prayed about who to ask, you seemed exactly the natural choice, because . . ." "With your artistic ability, you're a natural for the . . ." "You're such a good organizer, I know you wouldn't mind . . ."

If we say no to these requests, we feel guilty. If we agree, we then question whether it's the Lord's will. And who *always* knows God's will in anything? I like to think that the Lord directs my paths. But I'm not always sure that I'm responding to him rather than to the need or the immediate situation.

Each day God allows me twenty-four hours to spend. And many of those hours fill themselves with responding to human need. I'm a busy man, perhaps too busy. Perhaps I'm too busy looking at needs and seeing what I can do to alleviate those needs. Perhaps I spend too little time praying, "Lord, speak, for your servant hears."

I have no infallible way of knowing I'm making the right choices, but I pray and ask the Lord for guidance. Here are some simple steps I take:

Prayer comes first. *I ask, "Lord, is this a high-priority need?"* We generally assume that, because someone else stresses the significance of the task, it's a high priority item for us.

A few weeks ago another minister called me. One of our denominational colleges was beginning a capital gains fund, hoping to raise $100,000. Key leaders had been set up in all major areas. The leader for the Atlanta area called me.

"Cec, I know you could do a good job. We need a man of your commitment on the team. Will you help us by taking charge of the South Metro Atlanta area?"

"I'll pass this one by," I said, "but I appreciate your thinking enough of me to ask."

The other minister began to push. He told me of the importance of the college, the pressing need for additional facilities and for renovation. Finally I stopped him. "Look, I'm not going to yield. I agree the cause is worthy, but you'll have to find someone else."

He pressed again, this time commending my abilities to get a job done. Again I interrupted, "I'm simply not taking on anything new right now. The Lord and I have been talking over my schedule lately. And I've gotten myself committed to too many things. I'm backing off from anything new unless the Lord specifically tells me to get involved."

"In that case," he said, his voice softening, "I've got nothing more to say. I don't want you to go contrary to God's will." I believe he was sincere.

Second, try this prayer: *Is it a need I can meet?* All of us have limitations; all of us have areas of competence. For instance, no one ever asks me to do anything mechanical—in our church, we even joke about it. On the other hand, Arnold is one of the best handymen in our congregation. If you need anything done, from plumbing to carpentry to masonry, he's the man.

I recall a time when Arnold was asked to teach for two weeks in the Sunday school class where he is a member. He's a bright, articulate man, but no teacher. He tried to explain, but two other members insisted that he could teach. They finally arranged for someone else to take the second Sunday if Arnold would teach the first.

They never asked Arnold to teach again. He stumbled, fumbled, got twisted up in his words. It was an agonizing forty-five minutes for everyone—especially Arnold. But ask Arnold to plane a door or repair a leaky faucet, and he's right on top of the job.

Third, pray: *"Lord, do you want ME to do this?"* I've listed this third, but sometimes it should be the first prayer. Occasions arise when I'm aware that a pressing need exists, that I could do it, but that God doesn't necessarily want me to.

A year ago, we started prayer meetings in homes. In establishing the first group, we acknowledged the immediate need for a leader. I knew I could lead the group, and probably do it effectively.

"But should I, Lord?" The answer came thundering back: NO! We had two couples who were emerging as leaders in our congregation. As I prayed, it became quite apparent that the Lord wanted them to lead the group. What about me?

Three months later, we started a second prayer group. I led the first few meetings, but as I continued praying for guidance, I felt that the Lord didn't want me to be in that position. I backed off, and two more couples shared leadership.

It appears that's the way our home prayer meetings will go. As soon as approximately fifteen members attend regularly, we divide and form a new group with five or six of the original group. And each time, new leaders find their places.

What about me? I now visit among the Bible study and prayer groups. And it's exciting to me that several people are doing what I was tempted to do. The simple fact that I'm capable doesn't mean the Lord wants me for every task!

Finally, pray, *"Lord, give me peace in knowing I've made the right decision."* Have you ever made a decision and then for weeks afterwards wondered if you'd been right or not? Have you ever volunteered for a job, then looked back and cried, "Lord, did I run too fast?" Or have you refused a task, only to be tormented with thoughts that insist, "You really fouled up that time!"?

No one makes a perfect score in life—not even in seeking

God's will. But we can ask for peace once we've made the decision. In some instances, I've realized in retrospect that I should have decided differently. That kind of awareness usually comes after it's too late to get out of an obligation.

What happens then? I pray, "Lord, forgive me for not reading your directions correctly. I've given my word, so let me do the best I can. And Lord, give me your peace as I complete the project."

Even when I miss the Lord's will in one particular situation, I can learn from my mistake. Next time I know I'll be more careful. I'll not let subtle pressure intimidate me. I've learned that God doesn't call me to meet every need. He only calls me to obey him.

Questions for Thought and Discussion

1. How do you feel about Greg, the young man who always went forward? Do you tend to smirk? Feel sorry for him? Identify with him?

2. This statement appears on page 110: "I wonder if many times we're not guilty of responding to a *need* when we need to respond to God's *will*." Can you think of at least one instance in your life when you did that? What kind of pressures did you feel? How did you finally recognize it was the pressure of the need and not the pressure of the Holy Spirit?

3. Read again the suggestions for avoiding the pitfall of responding to needs rather than God's will. Can these be helpful? Can you think of other prayers you might ask?

4. Can you always know when you've made the right decision? What are some of the ways you can know? Does the fact of having interior peace seem sufficient evidence for you?

5. What happens when you responded to a need instead of to God, and have already completed the task? Do you mope? Feel sorry for yourself? Get angry?

6. In this chapter I state, "I've learned that God doesn't call me to meet every need. He only calls me to obey him." Discuss this.

7. Do you believe God really wants to guide us by the Holy Spirit? How do you feel when you've made a wrong choice? How do you think God wants you to feel when you've made a wrong choice?

8. How do you feel when you get a yes answer to the first two suggested prayers but have no answer for the third? Providing time allows, how do you get the third prayer answered? Continue praying? Make no decision? Decide to do or not to do and say, "Lord, if I'm not right in this, stop me"?

14
Pray for a Miracle!

AT AN INFORMAL PRAYER SESSION, Sandra, almost in tears, said, "Please pray for a miracle. We're about to lose our house and I don't know how we're going to make the payment this month. John's company's been on strike for almost a month, and who knows when they'll get it settled. And we just can't make it on what's coming in right now."

We prayed for Sandra and John. Although the strike went on another week, they managed to work out an agreement with the mortgage company to pay only the interest until they were on solid financial ground again.

The other day I was thinking about Sandra and her request. She wanted a miracle. Did she get what she asked for?

I believe in miracles. In fact, it's hard to read the Bible and not come to the conclusion that miracles truly took place. I realize critics have tried to explain away many of the beyond-nature happenings in the Bible. My faith allows me to accept the Red Sea story, turning water into wine, the resurrection of Lazarus and Jesus, the jug of oil that didn't run dry during three and a half years of famine.

I don't mind praying for miracles. But sometimes we need to ask ourselves what constitutes a miracle. As I think about this, I can list four types of situations that come under the category of miracle:

1) *The instantaneous.* While these appear more frequently in the Bible, they seem to be the most rare in the lives of people I

know. But they do happen. For instance, my wife received instant healing. From a head-on car collision she sustained multiple broken bones, torn ligaments, and lacerations. Three days later, while lying in the hospital bed, she felt a warmth pass over her body. The next day she *walked* out of the hospital—recovered.

I know of one man who lay in a coma for several days with no hope given that he would ever recover. One day he opened his eyes and said, "Hello." The same day he asked for food.

Once I prayed for a six-year-old boy. He had developed speech at a normal age. Then, when he was four, an illness took away his ability to speak. His mother asked me to pray for him, and I did. While I didn't sense anything taking place, she phoned within an hour after I reached home. "Timmy started talking almost as soon as you left. He hasn't stopped talking since."

During our missionary days in Africa, financial needs arose often. As soon as we became aware of them, we prayed for the Lord to provide. In numerous instances, within two weeks we received a check from friends in America who had not known the need. A letter enclosed often said something like, "The Lord impressed me to send this money."

2) *The normal route.* One winter I had a severe cold which I couldn't shake. The most visible evidence was a hacking cough which didn't stop. I attended the prayer group at our church and several people prayed for me. My coughing had stopped by the time the service ended, and that was the end of my cold.

I could reflect on that occurrence and say, "I received an instant healing." Maybe that's what actually happened. Or perhaps the infection had finally run its course. In either case, after that evening I didn't cough again.

3) *The circumstantial miracle.* I remember an incident in Africa which I call a miracle, although the circumstances weren't anything that defied the laws of nature. I was driving along the road, when suddenly my generator light went on. I didn't know enough about a car then to realize what could possibly have gone wrong—but enough that when a red light blinks, I stop.

I sat in the car, wondering how dangerous it would be to drive the additional five miles to the nearest place where I "might" find a mechanic—and that was only a vague hope.

"Father, I don't know what to do. Please intervene." My praying was interrupted when I realized that an African had appeared at my car. Not only did I not know anything about a car (I learned a great deal in the next six years), but I also didn't know enough of the local language to explain my problem. It was a remote part of Kenya where few people spoke English. Having been in the country only a few weeks, I was lost after we got past greetings and simple requests.

I struggled with the words and used a lot of body language. He nodded and said in English. "This is simple. I am an assistant mechanic from Kisumu. I can help you." Within twenty minutes he had my car running smoothly, and I was on my way.

A normal happening? Yes. But a man appeared who possessed two unique qualities—he spoke English (quite rare for that part of Kenya), and he was a mechanic (even more rare). He appeared on the scene just as I needed him. Yet he did nothing that was unusual or abnormal for him.

The miracle, in my thinking, was his appearance at the moment of my need. Perhaps he only "happened" to walk by at that moment. But why not ten minutes earlier? Or an hour later?

In the book of Acts there's another highway occurrence of that kind—a normal happening, but in the miracle category. An officer from Ethiopia is riding in a chariot (see Acts 8). He's reading a scroll of the Old Testament. And where does he *happen* to be reading? From Isaiah 53. At that precise moment, he gives Philip the evangelist a ride.

"What are you reading?"

He shows Philip and then asks, "Of whom is this prophet speaking—himself or someone else?" He provided the perfect opening for Philip to tell him about Jesus Christ. And the Ethiopian turned to Jesus Christ that day.

The miracle was not anything defying nature; it was the

bringing together of a man hungry for truth and another man who could answer his questions.

4) *Sufficient grace.* Two incidents of healing that didn't take place stand out in the New Testament. Most important, of course, is the case of the Apostle Paul. He writes in 2 Corinthians 12:6–10 of a thorn in the flesh which most people assume meant some kind of physical affliction—anything from a physical disfigurement or epilepsy to severe headaches or eye trouble or frequent attacks of malarial fever.

Whatever the sickness (if indeed it was really physical), Paul finally says, "To keep me from being too elated by the abundance of revelations, a thorn was given me in the flesh" (2 Cor. 12:7). He prayed three times for release, and then the Lord said, "My grace is sufficient for you, for my power is made perfect in weakness" (v. 9). No miracle of healing for Paul, but God was with him, enabling him to live through his affliction.

Another example of healing that didn't take place is found in Timothy 4:20, in which Paul writes, "Trophimus I left ill at Miletus." There is no mention of miraculous healing such as that of Jairus's daughter, of the lame man at the pool, of blind Bartimeaus. Here, in fact, is no healing at all.

In cases like these, God promises only that his grace is sufficient. And sometimes that's the hardest miracle to accept. For me, this simply means that while God sometimes says no to our requests for his intervention, he also stays with us, enabling us to be strong enough to endure our trials and problems.

I immediately think of Christian martyrs: Stephen, a man stoned for his zeal and commitment; Bishop Ridley of England; Joan of Arc; John Hus from the Reformation period; Dr. Paul Carlson of the Congo or Jim Elliot of Ecuador—both contemporary saints. For them there was no divine deliverance, but always a sense of God's presence with them.

The question naturally arises: what kind of miracle do we pray for? For an instantaneous one? For one to work out of nor-

mal events? For God to give us sufficient inner resources to endure?

My answer is that normally I pray for God to intervene in our
circumstances. The *what* and *how* I gladly leave in his hands.
We're exhorted in the Bible to pray, not to dictate the way God
must answer.

At times, there can only be an answer of provision, such as
when I need money or a job. When the job is offered or the
money appears, then I know God has provided.

Part of the joy of answered prayer is in seeing the *way* God
answers. And he can answer two similar prayers in quite different ways.

For example, two of my minister friends found themselves in
financial trouble. I prayed with both of them. A week later the
Lord had answered: "The pastor at Lake Avenue Baptist underwent an emergency appendectomy and couldn't perform a
scheduled wedding. The family asked me and I did it. The
groom slipped me one hundred fifty dollars—the most I've ever
received at a wedding. What an answer to my prayer!" That
was Hank's testimony.

Oscar said, "I always take Friday as my day off. Last week a
counseling center asked me to do two group seminars, both last-
ing eight weeks—one on Friday afternoon and the other at night.
I'll get $200 for the seminars."

Both miracles, because both were answers to prayer.

Perhaps the great miracles are just those—God answering
prayer!

Questions for Thought and Discussion

1. What kinds of miracles are listed in this chapter? Can you think of other classifications?
2. Read quickly through the Gospel of Mark. Note every miracle. Under which of the categories would you list each? (Because of the sketchy details, some might fit under more than one category.)
3. How do you account for the fact that most miracles described in the Bible are the instantaneous kind, yet in our lives this appears to be the rarest kind?
4. Can you think of a personal experience that can be classified as an instantaneous miracle? How did you feel about the suddenness of it? Surprised? Awestruck? Confused?
5. The concept of "normal" miracle refers more to timing than any unusual events. Can you think of an experience you could put into this category?
6. In the area of the normal-type miracle, how do you know it wouldn't have happened anyway without prayer? How do you make a distinction? Would it be proper to say that through the eyes of faith all good events are God's handiwork?
7. Reflect on the "circumstantial" miracle. What characterizes that kind of miracle?
8. The story of Philip and the Ethiopian constitutes a type of circumstantial miracle. Can you think of others in the Bible?
9. Could you classify the healing of Peter's mother-in-law as a normal-type miracle?
10. Does God providing "sufficient grace" take the place of a miracle? Is that a miracle also?
11. At the end of the chapter, I asked several questions about

what kind of miracles to pray for. Then I answered. How would you answer these questions?

12. Do you agree that simply the fact of God answering our prayers is perhaps the great miracle of life?

15

Prayers He Didn't Answer

ONE NIGHT while we were serving as missionaries in Africa, our house was attacked by robbers. They broke in while we were asleep, meaning to steal whatever they could and, if necessary, kill us. Local Africans heard our cries for help and came rushing toward us. The thieves fled, taking almost nothing.

The following night during family worship our small son prayed, "God, kill the robbers or save them." Shirley and I chuckled over his clear-cut kind of praying. And perhaps for a child of four it was appropriate, although I suspect that many of us have prayed that radical kind of prayer many times.

I wanted the robbers to be converted, but I certainly didn't want to see them killed, because I believe God's love would have wanted them to have time to rethink their lives and perhaps repent. We never knew what happened to the thieves, but I'm glad that we don't ask God to kill all our enemies.

That's only one kind of prayer that we can look back at years later and say, "Thanks, Lord, for *not* answering." I've also come up with a few others:

One type I call *destructive prayers*. A couple in a church I was pastoring tormented me constantly with their complaining, bickering, backbiting, gossiping, and even lying. They caused more trouble than a hundred other people could have done in a concerted effort. At one point, when I felt I couldn't take the woman's devilment any more, I prayed, "Punish her, Lord; punish her according to her sins."

The Lord didn't answer that prayer. Instead, he worked in me, teaching me to love the woman and to understand *her* problems. Then, almost abruptly, they moved fifty miles away, and the problem was removed.

Another kind of destructive prayer comes to mind.

I was only a boy when World War II raged, and very little of the actual events meant anything to me in those days. But I do remember reading the headlines of the evening paper when I was in grade school. The war had begun to turn in the Pacific, and the Allied forces were now on the offensive. One leading army figure was shown, shaking hands with Chiang Kai-shek of China. The military man had said, "We'll kill all those dirty Japs for you."

I wonder how many people were praying what that general verbalized: "God, kill the Japanese." How much better it would have been if the prayers could all have been, "Lord, bring peace to the whole world. Save lives."

A second group of prayers that I'm glad God doesn't answer are the *self-centered, me-only prayers*. I'm not talking about all prayers we make for our own needs; God wants us to freely go to him with all that concerns us. What I'm talking about are those prayers that reveal an attitude like that of a small child who wants what he or she wants regardless of inconvenience or hardship to others.

They are the kind of prayers made by the student who never opens a text, never takes notes, only half listens in class, but then prays, "Lord, help me pass this test. Help me make a good grade." All the while others in the classroom have faithfully done their preparation and made themselves ready. It's not merely the desire for a passing grade that's selfish; it's the attempt to get at the expense of others what was not earned.

When the devil tempted Jesus (see Matt. 4:1–11; Luke 4:1–13), these were the kind of lures he held before the Lord: "Turn these stones to bread," the Tempter said. "After all, you're hungry. You deserve to eat." When Jesus refused, the devil said, "Here we are at the pinnacle of the Temple. Throw yourself down. God will send angels to catch you." When Jesus again refused, Satan promised, "I'll make you ruler over all the kingdoms of the world."

Jesus said no to all three temptations. He would not perform miracles purely for his own selfish reasons. He would not tempt God by putting his own life into jeopardy. He had no desire to rule without having earned the right.

There's a third kind of prayer I'm glad God doesn't answer: *unmeant prayers.* On occasion we've mouthed words because they were expected of us, but inside we've not really meant what we've said.

During my college days on a Christian campus, we frequently had ministers and missionaries as speakers, many of whom would exhort us to go into full-time fields of Christian labor. The missionaries, especially, seemed determined to challenge us to go to the foreign fields. Not infrequently, we'd close our chapel services with hymns such as "I'll go where you want me to go, dear Lord . . ." And as we sang, several people rushed to the front. Others straggled behind. Eventually about fifty percent of the student body went forward. If they didn't, they were often intimidated for not going.

I remember talking to one of the students afterwards. "I thought you planned on working in the field of music and Christian education in a local church," I ventured.

"Yep, that's right," he replied. "I don't plan to go to Africa or Asia or anyplace else. I just thought I ought to say I'd be willing to go." He winked and said, "I don't know what I'd do if I thought the Lord really wanted me to serve in India or Africa. And besides, it gets the missionaries off my back."

I've heard people pray and say, "Lord, I'll do anything for you, just ask." I've been thankful that God didn't ask—he wouldn't have gotten much from them.

Fourth, I'm glad God didn't answer my *unwise prayers.* At the time I prayed them they seemed all right, but I didn't always know the facts. I didn't have the advantage of God's omniscience.

Two years ago Ron had an opportunity for a job change, and everything looked perfect. I remember praying especially for the Lord to grant him the position. But he didn't get it. I was stunned. Ron had seemed so right for the job.

A few weeks ago Ron and I talked over that situation. "I'm glad now that I wasn't chosen. The job pays twice what I'm making now, but I know the man who's doing it. He's married to his office seven days a week. The company is expanding so rapidly he seldom has time to take a day off. I could so easily have ended up the same way. I'm happy where I am."

Fifth, the prayers I'm most grateful God didn't answer are the *prayers for an easy time.* God never promises us an easy time, and hardships are often the best way for us to learn.

I've written elsewhere in this book about my struggle with temper. It took the dramatic, humbling experience of hurting several people to make me cry out to the Lord to help me control my temper. In most areas of my life I can record my share of failures before success came.

Even in the matter of prayer, this is true. In my early Christian days when I had plenty of free time, I remember wondering why all Christians didn't pray regularly. As I matured, and experienced job pressures, heavy schedules, tiredness, occasional boredom—all those factors that make finding time for prayer difficult—I could be a little more understanding and far less judgmental.

A bonus goes along with that. As I became more understanding, I was able to be more helpful. I want to strengthen people when they weaken. Part of my ability to reach out comes from having had my own time of suffering.

In the past two years I have lost several people near to me: both my parents, my older brother, a nephew, and a brother-in-law. Prior to that time I had never lost anyone really close to me. While I had sympathized with others, I hadn't experienced real grieving. Suddenly grief was firsthand and it hurt!

God didn't deliver me, didn't make the pain go away, didn't make life simple for me. Now that I'm on the other side of that grief, I'm grateful for the experience. Now I can identify with other people when they lose someone close to them. I know what it means to rejoice with those who rejoice and mourn with those who mourn.

That lesson came strongly to me today. I saw a beautiful poster. Bright yellow flowers in full bloom filled up most of the space. Rain was falling on top of those beautiful flowers, and in the corner of the poster I read these words: "Growth takes more than love and sunshine."

Yes, growth also takes the rain. And I'm glad for the rainy seasons in my life, just as I am delighted about the sunny days.

Questions for Thought
and Discussion

1. In this chapter, I thank God for not answering my *destructive prayers*. Read Luke 9:51–56. Why do you think the two disciples wanted to destroy the village? Read Psalm 5:9–10. Do you agree with the prayer of the psalmist?

2. Have you ever prayed for something bad to happen to an enemy? How does Jesus tell us to pray (see Matt. 5:38–47)?

3. We've all prayed self-centered prayers—the kind that put our own good over the rights and feelings of others. Can you think of one time when you prayed such a prayer? For instance, have you ever lied, and then prayed not to be found out? How do you reconcile this in light of God's justice?

4. Skim through Matthew 4:1–11. Can you see how yielding to the devil would have been selfish on Jesus' part? If so, explain your answer.

5. Reread chapter 9 ("Seven Selfish Prayers"). What differences can you see between the kind of "selfish" prayer discussed in that chapter and the "self-centered prayer" described here?

6. Do you think the following fall under the category of unmeant prayers?
   (a) A hasty thanks for a meal while your mind is on something else.
   (b) Praying for God to give Arnold a promotion while knowing that if he gets it your job may be threatened.
   (c) Your one office antagonist is in the hospital. You hear that he or she may have a long-term illness. You pray for a speedy recovery.

7. Jephthah made an unwise prayer—a vow to the Lord

(Judg. 11:29–35). Read 1 Samuel 14:24–46. Do you think these two passages fit into the unwise category?

8. Read 2 Corinthians 11:22–29. Do you think that one reason God used Paul greatly was that he suffered so much? How effective do you think the Apostle would have been if he had not gone through all his trials?

9. Read Hebrews 5:8. Do you think that suffering is a *necessary* requisite for the full Christian life? Also read 2 Timothy 3:12.

10. Have you been tempted to pray for life to be easy? Share one prayer of this type.

11. Why do you think God never promises us an easy time in our Christian life? Do you think we ought to pray for persecution? For problems to come upon us?

12. If you're part of a group, pray for yourself and for each other that you'll not be continually looking for an easy time and also that you'll endure when you have troubles.

16

Be Careful
How You Pray

"I'M GOING TO HAVE IT," Anna said. "I'm going to get that new house. After all, God wants us to have nice things, and for us to be happy. So I know it's okay. Every day I keep praying, and we're going to get the house."

She added, "In the past we've been bad credit risks, but I know we can work this all out, even though it's going to be hard to make payments. We can do it because God's going to give us the house."

They got the house. They also got a lot of troubles they couldn't handle. Their marriage almost ended in permanent separation. Matt walked out three times during their two years in the Spanish-style ranch house. If they hadn't decided to give up the house, he probably would have gone out one more time and not come back.

And yet, Anna had spoken so often of praying for the house. I recall when the matter first became a possibility. She asked me to pray. A prayer group of which we were both members at the time also pledged support. We frequently prayed for both Anna and Matt.

They got exactly what they wanted . . . but then they had second thoughts about it.

There's a principle I see about prayer that cautions me to be careful how I pray: *I just might get what I ask for.* Once I get it, I may not be satisfied. Or I may be worse off than before.

Sometimes God gives us what we want—even though it may

not be his will. It's as though we're spoiled, demanding children, crying, "Give me what I want! I'm going to have it!" And perhaps God gives in like an indulgent parent. Or perhaps, in his wisdom, he lets us find out if we really want what we are demanding.

When I was in graduate school and finances were tight, my daughter Wanda wanted a pair of sidewalk roller skates. After all, other children in the neighborhood had skates. Her best friend, whose dad was also in graduate school, had skates. Almost everyone in her school had skates, too. But it was also a time when we didn't have money to spend on such items. We realized, however, how much it meant to her. By careful budgeting, we found a way of getting them for her.

She put them on, filled with excitement, and ran outside and skated three hours. Yet within a week she had grown tired of skates. I don't suppose she ever played with them more than three or four times after the first week. She got what she wanted —but then realized she didn't really want them after all.

There's a parallel to this in the Bible. After the Hebrew people began wandering in the wilderness, God provided for their food. After all, they never stayed in any one place long enough to plant and harvest crops. The Lord sent them a special kind of food which they called "manna" (literally, "What is it?").

Every morning—except on the Sabbath—manna appeared on the ground like frost or large snowflakes. The people collected enough each day (with twice as much on Friday) for food. They baked the manna. They boiled it. They ate it plain. They got tired of one kind of food. So they began to grumble, "Is that all there is for us?" And they made it quite evident they wanted something else—meat of some kind.

It didn't seem to matter that God had miraculously provided the manna. They thought about only one thing—they didn't want to keep eating the same food every single day. And they got their answer. God gave them exactly what they asked for. Moses spoke to the people, "You will have meat to eat. The Lord has heard your whining and saying that you wished you had

some meat and that you were better off in Egypt. Now the Lord
will give you meat, and you will have to eat it."

But he said even more: "You will have to eat it not just for
one or two days, or five, or ten, or even twenty days, but for a
whole month, until it comes out of your ears, until you are sick
of it. This will happen because you have rejected the Lord who
is here among you and have complained to him that you should
never have left Egypt" (Numbers 11:18–20, TEV).

They got their meat! God sent quails for the people to catch,
for they flew only three feet above the ground. We're told that
"no one gathered less than fifty bushels" (Numbers 11:32).
They gorged themselves. Then an epidemic broke out.

All the writer says is that the anger of the Lord was kindled
against the people. He says it that way because, in Jewish
thought, all things come from the hand of God; whether he
allowed natural causes to kill the people, as may likely have been
the case, or merely stopped their hearts from beating—it was
all God's action. And many people died at Kibroth-hattavah.

In some ways this sounds like a rather harsh story. But there's
also the warning: be careful how you pray; God just might give
you everything you ask for. The same principle comes out other
times in the Bible. God had always planned for the nation to be
a theocracy—which means a nation ruled by God, with no royal
hierarchy. After the people settled in the land, however, they
demanded a king. They said, flatly, that they wanted to be like
other nations.

God warned them of the cost: increase of taxes, seizure of
their sons as slaves and servants, their daughters as wives. But
the people didn't listen. They continued to demand and, finally,
God gave them a king.

The first king started out right—Saul the son of Kish. But he
went amok; David succeeded him, and then Solomon. From
then on it's a downhill story. Finally the people had so turned
from God that he allowed the Babylonians to destroy their cities
and carry them away as slaves. But the Hebrew people had gotten what they asked for: they had their king.

I retain the memory of one experience in which God gave me what I prayed for and I later had many regrets. Prior to my entering seminary, my work had been largely in the field of education. I had been trained to teach, and had taught in both public and parochial schools. I had taught elementary grades and college. During the six years on the mission field my work had consisted heavily of training pastors and evangelists. We even set up a systematic teaching-training program for Sunday schools.

Later I entered seminary. It seemed the natural step to go on for a doctoral degree and then teach on a college level.

How did it work out? Beautifully ... at first. My grade-point average was second in our class, and I was awarded a healthy grant for graduate studies. Then, quite to my amazement, I discovered that G.I. education benefits were still available—even though it had been fifteen years since I had been in college. Seven months of benefits remained, and the government kindly extended the benefits to cover one full school year.

On top of all that, a small church three miles away from the graduate school asked me to become a part-time pastor. We were able to rent a house for considerably less than other houses in the neighborhood had been renting for.

Everything came about, of course, as Shirley and I prayed. And we prayed long, fervently, and often, "Lord, make a way for me."

In the area of graduate school where I chose to work, they selected only three students each year—and that year they received twenty-seven applications! But they selected me as one of the three. It seemed that I was on the way.

But by the second week, the wonderful life took a dismal turn. For the first time in my entire life, I hated school. I couldn't seem to find myself in the school. It wasn't that the work was so hard, but one professor took an instant dislike to me (another first for me!) and made classwork extremely difficult. The entire routine of schoolwork turned sour for me.

I dropped out after one year and went into the pastorate full

time. I've never regretted becoming a pastor, and I'm happier
in this work than in anything I've ever done. But it took a lot of
pain and struggle to get me here.

We all go through experiences in which we tell God what we
want and then later regret that God answered our request. Here
are a few conclusions I've come to about this kind of praying:

1) *God often gives us what we demand.* Sometimes we pray,
"Lord, show me your will." In reality, those are only throw-away
words because in our hearts we're saying, "Father, I *know* this
is right, so give it to me."

2) *God wants to teach us through this process.* The Lord
wants the best for all of us. He wants to choose our paths for us.
And when he chooses, it's the right path. In my case, even though
I felt suited for the academic life and it seemed a natural path
to take, God didn't choose that direction for me. I chose it and
then asked God to stamp his seal of blessing on my decision.
Since then I've learned to be slower in declaring any next step
as his will. I've also learned that he wants what's best for me,
not what's good or what's appropriate.

During the year of graduate work, I became the pastor of a
church with a membership of thirty-nine, thirty-three of whom
were over forty-five. During those months with the church our
membership doubled.

However, that's not the real story. During that time God
hooked me on the pastorate. Until that time I had never con-
sidered myself as fitting into the role of a pastor. When the
church opened up to me I saw it more as an opportunity to meet
my financial needs than as a vehicle of ministry for Jesus Christ.

I've been a pastor since then and have never been so happy or
contented before. This is my niche. To think that I almost didn't
find it! But once I realized my mistake, the Lord could tell me
what he wanted in my life.

3) *There are always new beginnings.* That's one of the marvelous facts about the Christian faith. We can keep starting
over—again and again. Jeremiah phrased it so well: "The steadfast love of the Lord never ceases, his mercies never come to an

end; they are new every morning; great is thy faithfulness"
(Lamentations 3:22-23).

4) *Our lessons are evidences of God's love for us.* Sometimes
God lets us fall flat on our faces. It's like giving the Hebrews
meat or allowing me to go on to graduate work. Perhaps he
knows that some people have to learn lessons the hard way. If
the Hebrews had been really committed to God, fully obedient
to him, it would have been enough for God to say through
Moses, "No, my children." But for that multitude, a word wasn't
enough. They had to have what they demanded.

How many times have you fallen on your spiritual face? How
many times have you demanded a new job, a bigger house, a
sleeker car, or a brighter gadget, and then afterwards wished
you hadn't done it? Those of us who know that story have to
learn lessons of life the hard way. But even when we do, God still
loves us. He may let us go as far in our own direction as we want,
but his love never diminishes.

I really went wrong in demanding my entrance into graduate
school. But perhaps I also had to go through that experience to
find myself, to know what I really wanted out of life. Yet I'm
also convinced that God has easier ways to teach us. We don't
need to end up in the hospital with an ulcer (as I did!) in order
to discover what God really wants.

"The steadfast love of the Lord never ceases." While Thomas
Wolfe told us in bold letters, "You can't go home again," Jesus
keeps saying, "Return ... come unto me ..." God's mercies are
endless. With him, there are always new starting places.

What might have happened had I really turned myself over
to God directly from seminary and allowed him to have his way
without interference from my will? I don't know. I can't even
speculate on it. I can only say, "Thanks, Lord, that you've continued to love me and to accept me."

Most of all, I've learned to be careful how I pray—especially
when I pray about major decisions. I've also learned that ulti-
mately I really do want God's best for me, even though it might
not be the course I'd choose.

Questions for Thought
and Discussion

1. Read the introduction of this chapter again. Anna knew what she wanted and prayed until it came about. Is it possible that God answers prayers even when harm may come to us? Defend your answer.

2. Can you think of any places in the Bible where God answered a prayer that was obviously contrary to his will? Would granting the people a king (read 1 Samuel 8: 1–22) fall into this category?

3. "I just might get what I pray for. And once I get it, I may not be satisfied." Can you think of an instance in your life when you wanted something very badly, kept praying for it, and finally got it, only to be disappointed or unhappy? If so, share with the group.

4. Read Numbers 11. Did the people get what they wanted? Then what happened?

5. Read again my experience in wanting to go to graduate school. Do you think God *directed* my actions? *Merely allowed* them? That my desires were so strong I couldn't hear God's voice?

6. This chapter states that God teaches us through the process of receiving answers to prayers that aren't really good for us. How does this help us learn? What lessons have you learned through experiences of this kind?

7. Read Lamentations 3: 22–23 in several translations if possible. In your own words rephrase these verses. Now think of a particular situation in your own life in which you got what you asked for and regretted it. Apply these verses to that situation. Does this help you forget? To forgive yourself? To thank God for ongoing forgiveness?

8. Read Hebrews 12: 3–11 and Proverbs 3: 11–12. How does

this apply to our mistakes and failures? What does the word *chastening* say to you?

9. In a concordance, look up the word *return* in the Old Testament. See how many times God, through his prophets, urged the nation to come back to him. Several of you might do this in advance of the group meeting and share several instances with the others.

10. Think again of an instance in which you demanded and received your will. How did you feel afterwards about yourself? About God? What have you learned from that experience?

17

Prayer–
Cause and Effect?

DURING THE WINTER MONTHS we kept a large bottle of chewable vitamin C on our table. As part of our breakfast routine, we each took one. Vitamin C plays a significant role in the diet; at least, that's what our family has been led to believe. We like to think that adequate doses of that vitamin ward off sniffles, colds, and other minor infections. However, we haven't found any direct correlation between vitamin C and lack of colds.

On the other hand, when we were missionaries in Africa, we lived in a remote area with a limited variety of fruits and vegetables. We noticed that when we brushed our teeth, our gums bled. We started drinking orange and lemon juice every day. Sure enough, no more bleeding gums—except in the month-long period when the trees were dormant and we couldn't buy citrus fruits. In that case we found a direct correlation.

One of the problems with prayer is that people are always looking for a direct correlation—they want to see a direct line from petition to answer. This I call the utilitarian view of prayer, and I'm not opposed to it—after all, why keep praying if nothing happens? How long must we ask and ask and ask and get only silence for an answer?

Olive really carries this direct line of prayer to an extreme. For instance, only recently she called me on the phone. "On Tuesday, did anything extraordinary happen?"

While I was trying to think back, she hurried on: "It was about 10:30 in the morning, and you came to mind. I couldn't stop thinking about you. So I started praying. I must have gone on about ten minutes."

So far as I could recall nothing unusual had happened at 10:30 Tuesday. Olive was slightly crestfallen. "But I prayed for you, so there must have been something happening to you that needed prayer right then and there."

I couldn't answer Olive's question. Did her praying prevent a tragedy? Solve a problem that I would otherwise have been torn apart over? Who knows? And why spend an awful lot of time worrying over it? But Olive does! For her, there's always a direct cause and effect for everything that happens. Then she's depressed or confused when she doesn't always come out with satisfying answers.

The other day, a church member asked me, "Tell me honestly, do you really believe God answers prayer?" When I affirmed that I did, he said, "Do you really believe that we can expect God to do what we ask?"

I replied yes, with qualifications such as God's will. After my dissertation he said, "That's all I wanted to know. I'm now beginning to pray to God every day. And I sure don't want to get into this if God doesn't answer our prayers."

In this instance, the church member was teasing. But I suspect a lot of people put prayer strictly on a pragmatic level. Their theology hangs on the "I cried—he answered" syndrome.

Is that all there is to prayer? Hang in with me while I sidestep into a theological explanation:

After the Protestant Reformation, especially between 1520 and 1650, the Protestant churches went through a period of formalizing their creeds as they established their denominations—the Lutherans, the Reformed, and the Presbyterians, as well as the later-emerging groups such as the Anabaptists.

One of the theological terms that came into being and floated around was called "means of grace." It's not a term you'll find in the Bible, so don't try to look it up. One of my seminary professors defined the term something like this: "Means of grace are those things which Christ, working through the Holy Spirit, uses for the gathering of the elect, the edification of the saints, the building up of all kinds of spiritual gifts, and to lead the elect to their eternal destiny."

How's that in our thought patterns? Means of grace are those things which the Spirit uses to bring people to Christ, to strengthen them, to use them in helping others, and eventually to lead them into unbroken fellowship with Christ.

The giant thinkers teach that these "means" are instruments (to use their terminology) of grace that remove sin and renew sinners so that they become more like Jesus.

They're quick to add that these are means in *themselves*. They don't have value because they are used by certain people or employed at a particular time, or because they often take place in a church building. The theologians also admit that we have high-charged experiences in our lives which strengthen our faith and our commitment, but that doesn't make them technical means of grace.

These means are "continuous instruments" of grace. That's another way of saying they're not something for occasional use or that happens accidentally; they are God's channels to communicate his love and to draw us into closer fellowship.

Although the post-Reformation theologians disagreed among themselves as to exactly which items stayed in this category, they included some or all of these: (1) prayer; (2) Bible reading; (3) the preaching and teaching of the Word of God; (4) public worship; (5) the sacraments—water baptism and the Lord's Table.

Now we've finished the theology lesson. What does all this say to modern Christians who want to commit their lives to Christ, and who want prayer to become a vital part of life?

Means of grace are God-established ways that we can mature in our relationship to him. These open the door for closer fellowship with Christ. We may not *feel* anything happening, but the process is going on anytime we make use of these divinely appointed means.

That's tough to explain because we can't verify or objectify the results. True, we can point to specific incidents when, in the

midst of crises we have prayed and received dramatic answers.
But for most of us, most of the time, cause-and-effect cannot be
verified. Can anyone say, "I pray thirty minutes a day. That's
why I have this great job and make $40,000 a year"? Or, "I read
my Bible every morning for one hour, and have been doing it for
twenty-five years. Since then, I've never had any sickness—in fact
my health is perfect. It's all because I read the Holy Book every
single day of my life."

I do believe that the divinely appointed means of grace
strengthen my faith in Jesus Christ. As I pray and as I read the
Bible, something goes on inside me. I may be absolutely unaware
of anything happening. After all, when did you realize you grew
from three feet to five? It was an unconscious process, but a
process going on all the time which no one doubts.

For me, the matter of prayer in life centers around asking this
question: If God has appointed tools by which we can mature,
why not use them? I maintain a daily prayer time for a variety
of reasons, but the overarching reason is that I'm convinced it's
an indispensable ingredient for spiritual maturity.

I want to grow. I want to live a contented, victorious life. Being
a Christian means being someone on the way—not a person who
has arrived, but one getting qualitatively better all the time. The
Apostle Paul says it like this: "Those whom God had already
chosen he had also set apart to become like his Son." (Romans
8:29, TEV). But I'll not keep on making progress toward being
like his Son unless I follow the rules of the game. That means
using the divine tools.

I learned a lesson about my body last year. After several weeks
of constant exhaustion, my doctor put me through a six-hour glu-
cose tolerance test. He told me, "Mr. Murphey, you have hypo-
glycemia—low blood sugar." He didn't give me any medication,
but he did put me on a strict diet.

In my case the diet was not to lose weight, but to regulate my
eating. Previously, I liked to be up a long time before I ate. Now,
as soon as I get out of bed, I head for the kitchen and a glass of
juice. I have three snacks a day. And I'm feeling better.

I also had to cut out one thing—I've been a confirmed coffee drinker for years and he said, "Caffeine is poison to you." The result: I've changed many of my eating habits, and my body has responded by being healthier. I have a normal amount of energy once again. But I had to do it the doctor's way!

That's the real secret to spiritual growth, isn't it? Doing it the Lord's way. And he's laid out the ways available for us if we want to mature.

Last week we had several needs in our church family. Judy underwent surgery for her back. Elderly Mrs. Moody was rushed to the hospital for anemia and possible heart problems. Mike had just received notice that his company was relocating in a distant state, and he didn't want to leave our church. Randy and Janet attempted a reconciliation in their marriage after three months of separation. All of these needs loomed before me, and I prayed about them each day.

But all my prayer time wasn't spent petitioning the Lord for their needs. Part of the time was in fellowship and giving of thanks. This week things are going smoother, and demands are less apparent. But I'm still praying even though I'm not as conscious of a lot of needs.

I can't think of prayer as so utilitarian that its only purpose (or even its primary purpose!) is what I get out of it! Nor do I pray only to get prayers answered. That's part of the package—and it's exciting to see how God actually answers our requests. But I also pray when no apparent needs occur to me.

We want to mature as a Christian. It's through praying, reading the Bible, hearing the Bible taught and preached, and worshiping with others that Jesus Christ ministers to us through the Holy Spirit.

Questions for Thought and Discussion

1. Are you familiar with the term "means of grace"? Someone might look up the term in theology books and bring in a report with a fuller explanation.
2. The author cites five "means of grace" on page 143. Ask yourself and members of the group how these help us grow toward Christian maturity.
3. Which of these means do you use the most? The least? Share with the others.
4. Do you always look for a direct cause and effect in your prayers? Anytime you have a good experience, especially one quite unexpected, do you look back for a specific prayer that preceded it? Why or why not?
5. Picture yourself as Olive in this chapter. How do you think Olive felt when I couldn't establish a cause-and-effect relationship between my situation and her prayer?
6. The author asserts that prayer is more than asking and receiving. What else is prayer?
7. Finish the following sentence for yourself, and then share it with the group. "If I want to continue growing as a Christian, I will have to . . ."
8. Can you think of an experience that shows a direct correlation between a need, someone's prayers, and God's answer? Briefly share.
9. Think of another experience of God's ministering to you in a situation where there was no direct, specific prayer offered. Does it comfort or confuse you to think that God doesn't always wait for people to pray before he intervenes?
10. For reflection: Why did God choose these particular ways of bestowing grace?

18

Divine Interruptions

"LORD, PLEASE HELP ME get this done for Thursday's meeting."

"God, no more telephone calls today. No more problems this morning, please."

"Father, it's frustrating. I can't seem to accomplish anything today. Every time I start working, someone barges in or the telephone jangles. I need just a few hours of uninterrupted work."

I know those prayers well—I've prayed them myself many times over the years. I suspect that most conscientious folks share the feeling.

It's not because we've been wasting a lot of time on previous days or procrastinating. In my case, I'm fairly well organized in my work, in my personal life, and even in my free time. It's okay for interruptions to happen when I'm not on a tight schedule, or when nothing urgent happens. But those aren't when the interruptions come! They always seem to hit when I have the least time to cope with them. Or perhaps they're always there, but I don't see them as interruptions unless I'm already involved in something else.

If the interruptions themselves were the whole problem, life wouldn't be so bad. They would only mean missing a few deadlines, or being late to a party, or not seeing ten exciting minutes of a TV film. But interruptions also spark other problems.

Such as resentment. A kind of why-me-at-this-time, Lord? feeling. I know my voice has shown that resentful feeling several

times, too; no matter what words I used, my voice and man-
nerisms were saying, "Don't people realize I have other important things to do?"

Interruptions also breed irritation. One fall afternoon the office
phone had rung off and on—it seemed continuously. I had pressing work to get done, so I decided to go home, hoping for a little peace there. But it was no better—I had a phone call inquir-
ing if I wanted to give clothes to the AmVets; a voice asked me
to subscribe to a variety of magazines for only pennies a day;
a woman from the Federation for the Blind sold me two cases
of long-lasting light bulbs. I turned down an offer to buy a ceme-
tery plot!

The first hour alone, I counted six phone calls—none of them
important. I was growling to myself, wondering whether I
ought to take the phone off the hook. Then it rang again.

"Hello!" I thundered.

After a long silence, a timid voice said, "I thought this was the
pastor's home. Sorry." And she hung up. I took the phone off
the hook for the next two hours and completed my work. The
woman, so far as I know, never called back. And I wondered
for a long time what she wanted and who she was.

That happened five years ago. Today, I've not totally won my
battle over this matter of interruptions, but I've come a long
way. I'd like to share some of the coping devices I've used.

Each morning I try to schedule my day. I make a list of what
I want to get done, as well as keep a pocket calendar of all the
things scheduled for that day. "Lord, help me know what I can
accomplish today and what I can't. Don't let me get frustrated
or irritated at interruptions." Praying and acknowledging that
the Lord has control over my life helps.

I do what I can to plan ahead, but I also allow him to break
into my life and change my schedule around. A principle has
finally gotten through to me: *People are more important than
things.* And "things" includes jobs, schedules, and my own plans.

I haven't always felt that way. I remember years ago when I
taught at a small college in the Chicago area. Because I lived

so far away and had an early morning class, I had to get up by 4:30 A.M. If anyone came to my house late in the evening, I simply did not let them stay long. I realize now that many times I was abrupt, rude, and so self-absorbed that I didn't hear their cries. I could think only of my sleep and the need to keep to my schedule. Naturally, I always explained why I had to go to bed, and no one ever said anything unkind to me. But I'm sure that I missed out on several opportunities to minister to people in need.

I recall that Don came by one evening minutes before I planned to retire. He was a slow-thinking, slow-talking kind, but also a man with a clear mind. He had been wrestling with the Christian faith for years. From time to time he would sit and talk with me about his doubts or his desire to believe. But one night he came too late, and I cut him off after ten minutes. I know the Lord's forgiven me, but I've sometimes speculated about what might have happened had I been willing to lose an hour's sleep. Don never came back again for lengthy conversations.

Another thing about my planning—I plan for divine interruptions in my schedule. I learned this during the time I was doing graduate work. It was a difficult time. Fresh from the mission field, I plunged into the graduate program at two different schools—carrying two full academic loads simultaneously. I handled that part all right, but it meant rigid scheduling of time for me. Whenever I found myself with even ten minutes of free time I used it constructively.

Each week I plotted my schedule for the next week, setting aside certain hours to study for each course. Those first few weeks I became constantly frustrated—I never could make it. Something unforseen always happened.

One happening was other students. They sometimes wanted to solicit my help in preparing for an exam, discuss a lecture, or just sit and have a cup of coffee together. I never became one of the time-wasters on campus, but I found a way to include these interruptions. I simply put it into my schedule!

Every day I allowed half an hour in the morning and another half-hour at night with nothing planned for that time. If people wanted to chat or study with me, I could make simple adjustments. Then when interruptions came, I could at least accept them as part of living.

That's been part of my lifestyle ever since. For instance, last Wednesday was one of those interrupting days. Most of the people in my congregation know about my writing habits and don't usually disturb me before 9:00 A.M. That gives me nearly two hours to write before my day as pastor begins.

But last Wednesday the phone was ringing as I opened the door. That call only took ten minutes. But I had barely gotten comfortable at my desk and inserted a sheet of paper into my typewriter when the phone jangled again. A distraught parishioner faced a real crisis and needed someone to talk to. After half an hour, she felt better; we prayed together and she hung up.

As I turned around to my typewriter, I looked up and saw one of the workers from a community agency. "Mr. Murphey, I'm sorry to bother you so early in the morning, but we have a family that desperately needs help. Their house burned down and we're trying to get them resettled and provide food and clothes."

When I finally turned around to my typewriter, I also glanced at my watch. It was nearly 10:00 and I had to make hospital visits before lunch. "Well, Lord, that was today. Please let tomorrow be more productive for my writing," I said as I got up from my desk. And Thursday was a productive morning—not a single interruption!

That's the way life is. I don't want interruptions in my schedule, but I accept them. At least I'm learning more and more to accept them as they come along.

And I'm learning to look for an element of serendipity in my life. *Serendipity* is a word coined by the eighteenth-century writer Horace Walpole. He wrote a story, "The Three Princes of Serendip" about three princes in Ceylon who made exciting discoveries. The word has come to mean making happy discoveries by accident.

During my student days I used to take long walks every after-noon. I lived in campus housing, which was located near several acres of trees and undisturbed beauty. Walking among the trees gave me a chance for a little exercise, as well as an opportunity to clear my head after sitting at a desk. Most of the time I spent in silent meditation as I walked. Sometimes I'd sing hymns of praise as I meandered through the trails. Occasionally, I'd take note cards with me to review principles and main points of text-books and lectures in preparation for tests.

One day, an elderly professor stopped me. "Every day I see you walking by yourself," he said in his thick German accent. "I also like to walk, and would very much like to walk with you."

I didn't know what to say. Inwardly I resented his intrusion. I had been able to commune alone with God, and now a stranger threatened to disrupt that time. But I said nothing of that to him. I simply responded, "Sure, join me."

And he did—almost every day for the next four months. Even on rainy days he met me at four o'clock, and we walked for three quarters of an hour. Over the weeks, we became friends. He was content to talk only if I wanted to talk. On several occasions we spent almost the entire time in silence. One time he brought a book on mushrooms and asked me to help him identify the edi-ble ones.

In time I learned to love the old man, and I realized how des-perately lonely he was. As the days continued, I began to feel flattered that he had picked me as a friend! I gained much from our relationship.

He died late that summer, only a short time before fall classes began. And for awhile I stopped taking walks in the afternoons. It just didn't seem the same without him. I still think of the old professor as a very special person in my life. But we never would have developed a relationship if the Lord hadn't broken into my life—if the old man hadn't asked to walk with me.

The logical conclusion to this chapter is that now I always

welcome the divine interruptions in my life, that I open myself constantly to God's breaking in and giving me new experiences. But the truth is, I still don't like interruptions. Scheduling and appointment-making remain part of my general makeup.

The Lord hasn't asked me to change that part of me. I believe he has been showing me that, when he breaks in, I should accept it and give thanks—not for the interruption, but for the fact that the Lord's always with me.

And ... sometimes I have to pray a few minutes before I can give thanks. Occasionally, I even complain to the Lord; after I've said my piece, he always seems to calm me down. I don't hear a voice, but it's almost as if he were saying, "Now, now, Cec. It's only a divine interruption in your life. You were getting too comfortable."

Once in awhile I've been able to recognize the divine interruption as it happens. Then I start out with saying, "Thanks, Father, for breaking into my life today." I wish I could always pray that prayer—at the very moment it happens. Who knows, next year or five years from now, I might be able to do that!

Questions for Thought
and Discussion

1. This chapter begins with three brief prayers for no disturbance. Do you find yourself praying this way frequently? Occasionally? Seldom?
2. Resentment and irritation are listed as common reactions to interruptions. Is that how you've felt? Or have your reactions been different? Have you felt anger? Hostility?
3. We've all been on the receiving end of these reactions when we've unintentionally interrupted people. Can you think of a particular instance in your life? How did you feel? How did you react?
4. I mention three things I have found helpful in learning to accept interruptions. What are they? Can you see how they could be helpful? Can you suggest additional helps?
5. In this chapter I mention learning to look for serendipitous experiences. Can you think of at least one experience in which an interruption that looked awful turned out to be a blessing?
6. If you're a person who carefully schedules activities for each day, how do you cope with the kind of people who want to talk endlessly and seem to have no concern about time? If you're the gregarious type who simply enjoys being with people and relating to them, how do you cope with the uptight individual who constantly looks at his or her watch and wants to dash off almost immediately?
7. Read again the experience of the student and the professor on page 161. Close your eyes and visualize the scene of their initial walk together. Which one of the two are you? Why?
8. How do you know if interruptions are *divine* interruptions? Or is every disruption divine?
9. Can you see danger in seeing every interruption as a divine interruption? Would it make your life one where

nothing productive gets accomplished? What dangers are there in being overscheduled and almost inflexible?

10. I say that I haven't learned to give thanks for the interruptions, only to accept them. Do you think it helps to give thanks for interruptions?

19
Preparing to Fail

NINA'S A DIABETIC with high blood pressure and six other ailments. She's also nearly sixty pounds overweight and unable to take off the excess. Nina takes her insulin regularly and keeps trying to do everything her doctor instructs. But she's failing— and she's doing that all by herself.

Each day she's preparing to fail both in licking her weight problem and in controlling her diabetes. For instance, one day I visited just as she finished icing a three-layer coconut cake. "Nina!" I blurted out before realizing my lack of tact. "You're not going to eat cake, are you?"

"Oh, this isn't for me," she smiled as she moved the cake to the center of the table. "It's for Jeff and the girls. You know I can't eat cakes, but they shouldn't have to do without."

I nodded, and the conversation moved on to other subjects. But in the back of my mind, I wondered. To her credit, Nina didn't take any of the cake while I was there. She didn't even glance at the contraband. But she did keep it in the center of the table, where it commanded attention from almost anyplace in the kitchen or living room.

A couple of days later, while I was visiting in the neighborhood, Nina's daughter Julie came over to see me. Julie was licking a double-dip ice cream cone. I kept teasing, asking for a bite. Finally I said, "Julie, you give me the cone. You can go home and eat that coconut cake your mother baked."

"Can't. It's already gone cuz Mommy ate half of it by herself last night while we were asleep."

I hadn't been prying for information, but I had suspected something like that. It didn't take any special insight to figure it out. Nina had set herself up to fail. Worse, she set herself up a pattern that led inevitably to failure. I suspect a lot of us do the same thing. We sometimes use more subtle methods, but we still prepare ourselves for failure.

For instance, we get ready for exams in school and say, "I'll never pass." Often, we're right. Or we stay up playing bridge until 2:30 Sunday morning, talking all the time about rising at 8:30 to go to Sunday school. Of course, we sleep until 11:15.

Another example: we know God honors a fervent, faith-filled prayer. So we pray, tacking on phrases such as "If it be your will, God." That saves us from having to examine the quality of our faith or the seriousness of our intentions. If we don't get a direct answer, we can shrug and say, "Oh well, it wasn't his will." Or maybe we just say, "Just as I thought—God doesn't really answer."

Sometimes the prayer goes like this: "Lord, I know I'm not worthy . . ." and then tell God what we want. If we get what we ask for, everything's fine. But if nothing comes of our prayer, we say, "Well, after all, I'm not worthy, so God didn't answer."

"I'll never do anything like that!" Such a boastful statement is an excellent way to prepare ourselves for failure. When Jesus said to the Apostle Peter, "You're going to deny that you ever knew me," Peter boastfully responded, "Not I, Lord! The rest of them might let you down, but not me. I'll *never* fail." As soon as he said, "I'll *never* fail," he set the trap for himself.

Don't be too hard on Peter. The other disciples claimed just as vigorously that they would stand with Jesus regardless of what happened. "We'll never let you down," they said. But when the opposition came, they were the first to run away.

Sometimes we fail because we become lax and quit trying. And people can manipulate us into failing. The Old Testament contains the story of man called Shemei—a first-class scoundrel. He cursed King David when the king fled from Absalom. Later, after David's death, King Solomon declared, "Shemei, you may live only so long as you stay within the gates of Jerusalem. As soon as you go outside the city, you have forfeited your life."

For three years Shemei stayed inside the city. Then one of his slaves disappeared, and Shemei went to get him. That meant leaving Jerusalem. He brought back the slave, but at the cost of his own death. Wise Solomon had set the man up to fail, knowing that Shemei would feel contented and safe and that one day he'd try to leave.

A lot of people have a hard time believing that it's okay to succeed—that it's even possible. You've probably heard of Murphy's Law. It goes something like this: If anything can go wrong, it will. That's asking for failure. Even though the law may be an attempt at humor, a lot of people live that way.

A friend of mine recently had trouble with her TV set. "Everything I get that's electrical is jinxed," she wailed. She'd had trouble with the TV, the clock radio, and the iron. But she forgot to mention that she hadn't had trouble with the refrigerator—now six years old—or the deep freeze, or her other TV, and she seldom changed light bulbs in the house. She saw only the failure syndrome—"I'll never be able to own anything electrical."

There are many ways of setting ourselves up to fail. But we don't have to keep on failing. We can change. Nina is a good example of this. She failed, but things turned around for her.

It started with a diabetic coma. Once she got out of the hospital, she determined, "I'm going to lick this thing." She told me; she told a lot of other people.

She accepted the fact that she was diabetic. It was an illness she wouldn't outgrow. She couldn't deceive herself by saying, "This one time's okay . . . just once."

Her family also came to her aid. The two daughters and her husband acted like the gestapo. "Mama, you can't have it. Not a single bite," one of the girls would say. And Nina discovered one of the most significant facts about winning over any problem: she needed support. She had at least three people to fight by her side.

To change our patterns of failure we have to change our whole way of thinking. We can concentrate on the positives of life. The Apostle Paul asserts, "I can do *all things* in him [Christ] who strengthens me" (Phil. 4:13). Jesus said, "With God all things are possible" (Matt. 19:26).

The Bible holds up treasures of promises, and even commands us to trust. So why don't we shift our thinking? Instead of setting ourselves up to fail, let's set ourselves up to succeed.

Here are two hints on how to do that: (1) Make this your constant prayer: "God, I believe you want me to be happy. I believe you want me to succeed. I believe you want to bless your people." You may need to pray that way fifty times a day. But keep saying it until you believe it. (2) The second prayer: "Lord Jesus, give me the necessary strength to succeed."

It doesn't matter what the problems; we can win over them. Like the Apostle Paul, we can learn to say and mean, "I can do all things in him who strengthens me."

Read that verse—Philippians 4:13. Read it several times every day. Each time you read it, pray, "Lord, make it a reality in my life." There's nothing automatic about success. You'll have a lot of obstacles along the way. But you *can* win!

Questions for Thought and Discussion

1. We all know people who can't conquer simple problems in life—controlling their gossip, drinking too much, overreacting. How do you feel about people who keep failing at problems you're not troubled over? Do you find it easy to pray for them?
2. How did you respond when you read that Nina ate half a cake during the night?
3. On page 156, I listed several possible times when people set themselves up to fail. Choose one of them—or a similar one you can think of—that you've used to help yourself fail. Can you think of the circumstances in which you deliberately fell into the failure trap?
4. Think of an experience in your life (you don't have to share the experience itself unless you wish) in which you prepared to fail and succeeded in the failure. What kind of feelings went through you? How would you have reacted if you hadn't failed? Did you secretly want to fail?
5. Why do people fail? The chapter suggests several reasons —boastfulness (as in the case of the Apostle Peter); laxness (as in the case of Shemei); addiction (to sugar as in the case of Nina). Can you think of other causes?
6. Can you recall one instance in which you actually overcame a problem after one or more experiences of failure? What happened to make the change? How did you change your attitude and your actions?
7. In Nina's case, her husband and two daughters provided support. So did her pastor and friends. How can this be a source of strength to people trapped by failure? Can you also see dangers?
8. Stop all talking. Either have each person in your group read Philippians 4:13 from the Bible, or have the verse

printed so everyone can see it. Each person should read
the verse slowly five or six times. Pick out three words that
speak most to you out of that verse. Then share.

9. Try this with Matthew 19:16. You may think of other
verses; follow the same procedure with them.

10. Concentrate on one area of your life in which you've failed
repeatedly. But make it an area that you'd like to see
changed. Share this need briefly with the others. (If you're
doing this individually, perhaps you could share with a
friend). Commit yourself to think of Philippians 4:13 every
time you're tempted to fail. Remind yourself to pray, "Lord
Jesus, give me the necessary strength to succeed." Ask at
least one other person to pray for you every day until your
group meets again. The next time your group meets, make
this the first matter of sharing.

11. Continue this process of (a) frequently reading/reciting
Philippians 4:13 (b) praying for necessary strength and
(c) asking a friend to pray for you each day. At the end of
three weeks, share with the others your experiences.

12. Think of the most serious recurring problem you have in
your life (bouts of temper, inability to handle money wisely,
inability to hold on to a job, etc.). Do not share this with
others unless you wish to. For the next week, look for tell-
tale evidence there that you have set yourself up to fail. Ask
God to help you see where *you* have chosen the failure
trap and it's not because "they" or "she" or "he" or anybody
else has done it to you. Make this a continued matter of
prayer each day.

20

You Can Change

WE'VE ALL HAD experiences of repeated failure. We want to change, but somehow we can't seem to make it. Whether it's giving up smoking, losing thirty-five pounds, becoming faithful in church attendance, or learning to control our tongues—the subject doesn't matter—change becomes a heavy battle for most of us.

Wouldn't it be great if we could say, "I'm going to change!" and everything went perfectly from then on? Unfortunately, life doesn't work out that way. I know folks who have struggled to change habits and then given up. "I'll never make it." Or "I'll always be the same. I can't change."

But I don't believe that; I'm convinced we can change! We can be different—just as different, or as improved, or as controlled as we really want to be. However, in order for change to be a reality, certain steps have to take place.

The first step toward change is *suffering*. None of us changes anything we're comfortable with. Until we become aware of how it hurts us or how we've hurt someone else, why change?

One of the most remarkable change stories in the Bible involves a man named Zacchaeus. It doesn't take much imagination to see suffering in the life of Zacchaeus. We're told in Luke's Gospel (19:1–10) that he was a tax collector. As a tax collector, he was assumed by most people to be an extortionist. Even though he was a Jew, his own people detested him. With all his money and the possessions he acquired, he didn't have friends or self-respect or peace with himself. That's real suffering. But it led him to go see Jesus. And we know from the biblical account that he went in the house with Jesus a rogue and came out a saint. He was a changed man.

Remember the story of Joseph from the Old Testament? Originally, he was a nasty kid—always parading around his revelations from God, always displaying a superior attitude toward his brothers. And being the obvious favorite of his father Jacob only fostered his attitude.

Then Joseph went into servitude in Egypt. There he eventually prospered, but not before he had undergone much suffering. I've wondered if he didn't suffer just as much internally, rethinking how he had caused his brothers to hate him. We do know that after he found favor in the king's eyes he was a compassionate person.

Last year, six people in our church gave up smoking at approximately the same time—all of them people with the habit formed over many years. They shared with me their reasons for quitting. One realized how much she was spending—more money each month to feed her habit than she spent in food for her baby. Another was developing a hacking cough and knew he was doing harm to his body. But whatever their individual reasons, they *did* quit. And each of them suffered in some way before making that resolution.

That's how we have to start if we're going to change—we have to suffer enough to want to do something about it. If the word *suffer* sounds too strong, replace it with words like *frustration, failure, guilt*. Or perhaps, say that one is sick of repeating a type of behavior. It's the kind of feeling that compels us to pray, "Lord, make me different." Perhaps Paul's prayer in Romans 7:24 is appropriate: "Wretched man that I am! Who will deliver me from this body of death?"

The second step toward change is *insight*. That's when we know a change is possible. It's an awakening hope that says, "I can do it." It's the inner voice that assures, "I don't have to wallow in guilt or self-pity."

I've seen several people make their commitments to Christ at a stage like this. They're sick of their old way of life, tired of being miserable. Then they realize that Jesus can help them change.

One of those people is Madge. One afternoon she awakened out of an alcoholic stupor. Her house was in shambles. As she began to put events in order in her mind, she realized that three days had been lost—three days for which she couldn't give an account. She looked into the bathroom mirror and screamed, "What am I doing to myself?"

That was the point of change in Madge. At that moment, she remembered a verse she had learned as a child in Sunday school: "Come to me, all who labor and are heavy laden, and I will give you rest" (Matt. 11:28). And from that moment, her life took a different direction.

Third, after insight must follow *the desire to change.* Here's where prayer comes the most sharply into focus. For many, prayer becomes the last reach for help. We try prayer when we realize our sense of helplessness. But we also pray because there's the beginning awareness that things can change.

The life of Peter shows this clearly. He was a quick-to-jump fellow, always speaking up before he had a chance to think. Yet he had a boldness that, once God-channeled, made him into a great apostle and leader.

It seems to me that the point at which God really got through to Peter and made him want to change, was when he denied Jesus. Jesus had predicted, "Peter, you'll deny me," and the fisher had adamantly replied, "Not me!" Yet that very night, in the presence of a young maid, the apostle swore he didn't even know Jesus.

The Gospel of Luke ends the account this way: "And the Lord turned and looked at Peter. And Peter remembered the word of the Lord, how he had said to him, 'Before the cock crows today, you will deny me three times.' And he went out and wept bitterly" (Luke 22:61).

That was the turning point for Peter—he went out and wept

bitterly. It was a moment of giving up, and yet he must have also, at the same time, been crying out for change in his life. Judas killed himself, but Peter went fishing. That's how I see the difference when the two men confronted themselves. One man simply gave up life. The other, although discouraged, kept on.

The last step—the actual change—is to *take action*. For Zacchaeus this meant restoring money. For Peter it meant becoming a man of strength and going with the others to pray in the upper room. For you it may mean putting a curb on your tongue, or starting to handle money wisely, or getting up when the alarm rings, or learning to pray for rude drivers instead of wanting to curse them. If the first three steps have been followed, liberally doused with prayer, step four is possible. But the desire to change has to be strong—not merely "I wish I were different."

For my friend Gene, change meant forming new thought patterns. He says, "I've always been a negative person. Most people would see water in a glass and say it's half full. All I could ever think of was that the glass was half empty." Gene criticized other people's actions, found fault with coworkers, and wondered why he was never asked to serve in leadership capacities at church.

Then came an experience that was painful for Gene: his company passed him over for promotion. The department head said, "Gene, there'll be other opportunities if you're ready for them. But we need leaders who can enthuse others and are excited themselves. We want people who can encourage and not tear down."

Gene says, "After a week of feeling sorry for myself and praying about it, I decided I wasn't going to stay Mr. Negative." Gene was quality controller of one branch of the plant. He constantly inspected the work of dozens of people. "I got tired of being disliked at the plant. Some mornings I'd walk through, feeling everyone was against me. So I began praying for the Lord to help me understand the people as well as the work."

Gene changed. For him the real moment of change came

when he took concrete action: he began treating other people with kindness. "At first I felt like a hypocrite. A couple of times I wanted to yell out, 'You dummy!' But I didn't. After a week or so, I discovered something—I really had changed. I am different now. Now, when I inspect, I always look for something good. No matter how badly done a job is, I try to appreciate something. Only after I've been able to commend the good do I point out the discrepancies."

No matter what it is that bothers you about yourself, you *can* change. The Lord wants to make us all free; Jesus Christ is always waiting to help us change. It's up to us to want to!

Questions for Thought
and Discussion

1. Near the end of the chapter is Gene's story. Put yourself in his place prior to his change. What does it feel like to be pessimistic about people and life? How do you think you feel about yourself?

2. Gene made a commitment to be different. Can you put yourself in his place? If you're part of a group, tell some of the specific things you would do to make lifestyle changes.

3. Read the story of Jesus and Zacchaeus in Luke 19: 1–10. Let your imagination decide what happened to Zacchaeus to make him return money and goods he had defrauded.

4. Go through the chapter and read again the steps for change. Sometimes these steps overlap, but try to see them as distinct. Then read Romans 7: 1–24 along with the story of Paul's conversion (Acts 9: 1–20 or 22: 4–16 or 26: 9–18). See if you can fit in the four steps in this chapter.

5. Another biblical character mentioned in this chapter is Joseph. Skim through Genesis 37–45. Can you see where the four steps fit?

6. From what you know of the Apostle Peter, can you see how he changed from one kind of person to another? Compare the attitude of the man in Gospel accounts with that of the man who preached in Acts 3, 10, or 12.

7. How much does change depend upon the Holy Spirit, and how much upon ourselves?

8. Do you know people who have made drastic changes in their lives for the better? If so, describe the changes as you see them. What about your own life? Can you look back over the past five years, or even the past six months, and see changes? If you answer no, can you think why?

9. Pause now and pray silently for one area in your life that you want changed. After prayer, briefly tell your need to another person who will pray for you.

21

Reporting for Duty

ALL OF US were in our twenties—all eager to serve Jesus Christ. We had heard the speaker tell of heroic adventures in Japan, of Christian perseverance in the face of great danger. We had listened to tales of hardship and bitter opposition.

"And you—you young people! Won't you give yourself to God's service?" The speaker challenged us with the kind of appeal to which idealistic youth respond—adventure, danger, excitement. "How many of you will give yourselves to Jesus Christ to serve him on the foreign fields of the world?" he asked several times.

After a few more minutes he started us singing a missionary hymn—"Where he leads me, I will follow . . ." My wife Shirley and I sat listening, certain our call to service did not include the foreign missionary field. Yet the music stirred us, and the speaker's high-intensity message captivated us. He pleaded for us to come forward, adding, "Commit yourselves to him. Won't you say, 'Lord, I commit myself to the mission field, unless you show me I'm not to go'? Will you pledge to go unless God expressly forbids you?"

I moved forward then, positive that foreign missions wasn't God's plan for me. And even though Shirley and I eventually spent nearly six years in Africa, I don't believe our time in the mission field had any direct connection with that night.

What was important about that evening is that we made a commitment of our lives to Jesus Christ. "Lord, use me," I remember praying as I knelt at the front. Shirley was praying silently, "I'm yours, Lord. Use me as you see fit."

As I knelt there, I thought of myself as a soldier for Jesus Christ. I didn't have a vision or any trance-like experience. Instead, having been discharged from the Navy only a few months, I thought of my previous four years in the military.

I had joined voluntarily. I had made my commitment to the Department of the Navy. From then on, a higher power made decisions for me. I could make requests, and have hopes or desires, but I didn't have the power of choice about where to serve or what kind of duty I wanted.

I recall thinking, as I knelt at the front of that auditorium, that I was reporting to Jesus Christ. I was standing in the line of muster: "Cecil Murphey reporting for duty, God."

That's what each of us did, in effect, as we marched down that aisle to the front. We surrendered—or at least some would have stated it that way. I didn't like that term. For me, surrender meant saying, "I'm tired of fighting you, tired of arguing, so now I give up."

I think that's what happened to Carl, who sat next to me. He had come to the service with us. There is no question in my mind that he was a Christian, and that he wanted to serve Jesus Christ. But Carl had not grown to the point that he was able to make an all-out commitment. I had seen the struggle on his face during the early part of the message—wanting to give in but still fighting God's call.

Knowing Carl's nature, I imagine he carefully weighed the cost to him. It was considerable—a certain parting with his family, who were nominal church members and very much against this heavily-accented religious emotionalism; the possibility that his many friends would drop him. Finally, as the missionary continued his fervent pleading, Carl went forward. For him it meant a new direction in life. He had reported for duty, saying "I'm in your service now, Lord, without reservation."

When I stop to think about prayer and the Christian life, this fact stands out more and more. Prayer implies an unquestioning obedience to God's will. Of course times occur when we're not sure, when we're confused, when we need courage to carry out his will. But for the Christian, coming to Jesus Christ in face-to-face encounter means saying, "I surrender, Lord. I'm reporting for duty."

Now, a soldier of the cross can always go Absent Without Leave. A Christian can always run away. And plenty of God's people have done that. Jonah is a classic example. He ran from God's will because "I knew that thou art a gracious God and merciful, slow to anger, and abounding in steadfast love, and repentest of evil" (Jon. 4:2). He knew that when he preached the message of God's impending judgment the Ninevites would repent. And because the Hebrews were long-standing enemies of the Ninevites, Jonah wanted to see that nation destroyed. So he ran rather than submit.

Some people run away out of fear—like Elijah. After a marvelous victory over the priests of Baal, we would expect his life to have run smoothly. But Queen Jezebel, in her fury, sent out word for the prophet's execution. And he ran. There was a day when he stopped running and listened to God's voice again. He received new courage and returned to where God wanted him. But for a brief time, even the bold prophet went A.W.O.L. in the face of the enemy.

Sometimes when we report for duty we need reassurance of God's directions. Peter had fished all night and caught nothing with his nets. Then Jesus said, "Throw your net overboard one more time." Peter knew it wouldn't do any good. An expert fisherman, he probably knew more about fish than the one trained as a carpenter! But he wasn't talking with just any person. He was talking with God's representative, the Messiah.

"Okay, I don't think anything will come of it," he must have grumbled. "Nevertheless, at your word . . ." Peter threw the net over the side of the boat and captured the largest haul of fish he'd ever had. He had done as Jesus commanded.

When I first came to God, my prayers focused on God's

existence: "If you're real, hear me." "God, if there really is a God, make yourself known to me ..."

Those days brought me into relationship with him. Then came a change—I knew he existed. I believed. And the whole relationship changed, even my prayers. I prayed, "Teach me to know you." "Make me obedient." "Guide my life."

Those initial prayers bring us to Jesus Christ, but our prayers change after we commit ourselves to him. This was true for the boy Samuel. Once he knew the Lord was speaking to him in the ancient temple, he replied, "Speak Lord, for your servant hears." He was reporting for duty.

Isaiah's real usefulness began after he had a vision of God's majesty and holiness. Then he cried out, "Here am I, Lord, send me." Again, reporting for duty.

One time a Roman soldier needed help: his servant lay critically ill. He sent another servant to Jesus with a message—"Master, if you just speak the word, my servant will recover." That's the kind of faith Jesus commended. He held up the non-Jew as an example to the disciples around him. "Why, I've never seen such faith as this before."

That's the kind of faith we exhibit when we report for duty, awaiting our orders, ready to move forward.

Questions for Thought
and Discussion

1. Close your eyes. Visualize yourself in a military uniform standing in line with Jesus Christ the commander. As he walks down the line, he looks at each person, says something to each of them (which only that person hears). He now stands before you. What does he say to you? Share this with the group.

2. Picture yourself as Jonah, who heard the command to go to Nineveh but decided to go the other way. Why have you chosen to disobey? How do you feel as you board the ship to leave your homeland? How do you feel when the whale swallows you? When you've been vomited up on the shore?

3. You're Elijah. Previously you've been bold, but this time you're running from Queen Jezebel (read 1 Kings 19 for details). Why are you afraid? What does it take for God, your leader, to assure you of his protection?

4. Visualize yourself as Peter (see Luke 5: 1-11). How do you feel when Jesus tells you to try your nets one more time?

5. Can you recall an experience in your own life when you "reported for duty"? What events led up to this decision? Briefly, share with the group feelings you had then.

6. Think of three words used in this chapter: *duty, obedience, surrender.* How do you see them as different? As similar?

7. This chapter contains the statement, "Prayer implies an unquestioning obedience to God's will." Do you agree or disagree with that statement? Share your views.

8. Visualize Jesus as the commander passing down the line again. This time each of you says something to him. Now he stands before you. What are you saying? Share this with the others.

9. This chapter views the Christian experience in terms of the military life. Try thinking of it according to other biblical

models. What about a father and his children? A master
and his slaves? A mother and her infant child? A mother
hen and her chickens? Do these help give you a better view
of the Christian life?

22

No Such Thing As Happily Ever After

"I'LL NEVER BE THE SAME AGAIN. Never." With tears streaking her mascara and several once-curled locks of hair now hanging limply, Vera said, "The Lord has really changed me. I'm a new person." And Vera did change. For the next three months I don't think I ever heard her gossip or grumble.

Those had been her greatest weaknesses—a sharp tongue and a negative attitude. Vera had always had the last word about everyone:

"I've been in this church twelve years. No one ever asked *me* to be president of the Women of the Church. Gail's been here less than a year, and look at her—she's already taking over and she'll be the next president. Wait and see."

Then came a series of meetings with an emotion-charged but honest-dealing preacher. He called a lot of us to commit our lives to Jesus Christ without reservation. On the second night, Vera responded. And when she walked away from the front, despite the ruined makeup, her face had a beauty I'd never seen before. "You even look different, Vera," I said.

"I am different. I'll never be the same again. Never!" She meant it.

But within a year Vera had begun slipping into her old ways again. Perhaps she was not quite so much a grumbler (although I'm not sure about that), or quite so critical about people. But basically she went back to the same lifestyle I had seen before.

Vera's no isolated example. Others have had their lives turned around by Christ, only to return to their old habits in a few months. Why doesn't the change last?

Last year we discussed having a week of "revival" meetings at our church. "We haven't had one for three years or so—not since before you came, Mr. Murphey," Harold said. "Maybe it's time to have one again."

Andrea hardly let Harold finish before she said, "Oh, let's not have one. I've been going to our revivals for twenty-five years. What happens? A man comes in and he's good—really good. He stirs people up. They confess their sins and make all kinds of promises. And two months later they're back doing the same things again."

The discussion lasted another ten minutes, but Andrea had closed off the arguments. Several agreed with her. Even Harold, who wanted to see such a series of meetings, had nothing to say in rebuttal.

As I sat there during the discussion, the question kept floating around in my head: Why? Why is this so? The evangelist or preacher proclaims a message out of true commitment. God declares that his Word doesn't return fruitless. Certainly people today are basically the same kind of people we've always had in the world.

I began thinking of experiences in my own life, especially my commitments or moments of intense dedication. I had prayed, surrendered everything to Jesus Christ. I expected, for that part of my life at least, to live happily ever after.

Then I discovered what, for me, became a significant liberating truth: There is no such thing as "happily ever after." We solve a problem—wonderful. Life changes. And then next week or next year we're stuck with other problems—sometimes even greater problems than before.

This has happened in several areas of my life. My bout with temper stands out as a significant example. It's easy to say I have always had a temper—most people do. In my case, the fires of anger usually took a while to heat up. But once the fire erupted, I shouted with unreasonable demands or assertions. Then it was

over and I calmed down. But I was always like the volcano—
subject to eruption at any time.

While I served on the mission field, God delivered me from
the awful temper. I felt like a new person, one who would never
scream or rage or shout again. And I didn't get really angry for
at least four more years. Then I had only minor blow ups—
minor compared to my earlier temper. I had won the battle; God
had delivered me. *Or had he?*

Only a few years later my temper erupted again. I don't know
if it was as intense or not—after all, when you lose control, the
degree isn't terribly important. The situation had been smolder-
ing for at least a year, and I had carefully said nothing. Problems
and awkward situations kept developing, and in most of the
instances the cause could be traced back to Hal and his wife Faye.

The list of their sins staggered me. They called themselves
Christians—Hal even served as an elder—and yet they gossiped,
lied, and used any underhanded method available to accomplish
their purposes in the church. One of Hal's favorite ploys was to
make an accusation starting with "Some of the people in this
church are saying . . ."

In a board meeting, we were discussing a particularly delicate
problem. Hal stood to his feet and said, "Mr. Murphey, I don't
think that's a very good idea. Several people in this church are
saying . . ."

I didn't even let him finish. "Hal, right now we're not talking
to several people of the church. And we're not going to base our
decisions on what you think they might be saying."

That silenced Hal. After all, no pastor had ever talked back to
him before. But the next morning, Faye called on the phone.
"Mr. Murphey, I resent the way you spoke to my husband in
the board meeting last night." She went on for a few seconds,
but I didn't hear any of her words.

I simply exploded. "Faye, I only wish you had been there, too.
I would have told you that I think you're underhanded sneaks
and marvelous tools of the devil!" My voice kept hitting the
higher registers, and I climaxed it with, "You two have done

everything you can to sabotage the work of the Lord in this church!" She hung up.

So far as I knew then (or even now), every word I shouted was true. I could even document my information. But I felt terrible. I had lost control. Yet I had thought the Lord had delivered me from my fiery temper. "Remember, Lord? You set me free from this once."

Over the years I've still struggled over control. The battles are less intense, and failures creep in less often. But it's an area that will always demand prayer and watchfulness.

God's setting me free from temper was a victory—but one victory doesn't necessarily win an entire war. It simply brings me one step closer to ultimate victory. Other battles lie ahead yet. But God answers our prayers. He gives his guidance and his strength.

In this almost life-long struggle with my temper I've discovered a few approaches to prayer that help me:

1) *Preventive Measures.* When I realize touchy situations are coming up, I can fortify myself. Certain people or particular situations lend themselves to tensions, temper flare-ups, and trouble.

"Lord, guide all of us in our board meeting tonight. We're going to discuss fund-raising projects. We already have two distinct attitudes at work. Help me keep calm. Help me control my temper."

Another tactic: I pray for the individuals involved. With most people I get along fairly well; however, a few people, by their very presence in a room, irritate me.

Elizabeth, for instance, always brings out the worst in me. I can reflect, out of her presence, and say, "She's manipulative, demanding, and stops at nothing to get her way." But then, I've known other people even more cutthroat, and while I didn't want their close friendship I didn't feel the same irritation stirring in me.

I can think of two other people like Elizabeth. The reasons I feel uncomfortable with them may not be important. But by praying for them and for our relationship when we're going to be together, I've been able to come away feeling much better as a person and as a Christian.

2) *In the Situation.* Here's the trouble spot, but I'm learning. Sometimes I sense a physiological response to anger. I can feel a tightening of my muscles. My breathing becomes labored and, if I'm really getting upset, my voice sounds shaky. Those signs usually are enough to make me back off. I silently pray, "Lord, I'm losing another battle. Fill me with your peace and love now." I'm learning to listen to myself and to accept God's help in the midst of struggle.

Sometimes I'm able to back away from the situation and reflect. At a meeting of our Christian writers' group, Gary kidded me several times. Then one of his barbs hurt.

I almost lashed back at him. Then I started praying for the Lord to help me. I also asked myself, "Why am I getting upset over this?" Within five minutes I had cooled off, realizing I had been extra-sensitive. I was ready to involve myself in the discussion again.

Immediately after the meeting closed, Gary said, "I hurt your feelings, didn't I?"

"Gary, I was angry. It took me a few minutes to realize why I got upset, but I'm okay now."

Another helpful thing: I'm admitting that I can only get hurt, angry, or upset in the "unsettled areas" of my life—areas where I'm still sensitive or uncommitted. The battles rage where victory hasn't really been won. Keeping track of situations that upset my spiritual balance makes good prayer material!

3) *After-the-Fact-Measures.* I still lose control once in awhile. It doesn't happen often—at least not with the frequency it did twenty years ago! Naturally, I always feel remorse or guilt after every instance in which I lose my temper, even when it didn't show. I don't think anger in itself is sin; the handling of it is what matters. The Apostle Paul said, "Be angry and sin not" (Eph. 4:26). I find, however, that unresolved anger smolders,

until one day it erupts. I want to fight it from becoming destructive or harmful. These are some tactics I have found helpful:

Asking the Lord's forgiveness comes first. If the other person realizes (or has cause to realize) my anger, I apologize—once the Lord gives me victory.

Here's something I've found helpful in my own battle. I call it Fantasy. First, I replay the action in my mind. And every time my antagonist speaks, I play "one-upmanship" with him or her. I always say the clever word or make the devastating remark, and always come out on top.

Then I play Fantasy from the other end. The person decimates *me*. I'm the victim. Poor little me. I remain quiet, humble, long-suffering. My persecutor walks all over me. Then I smile and say, "May God's peace be with you." I am the martyr, and I win by submission and humility.

When I've finished with both my versions of Fantasy, I realize that neither stance was healthy. But I've said all the vengeful things I've wanted to say; I've gotten it out of my system. Or I've played the sweet little long-suffering Christian.

Now I look at the situation and try to find reality somewhere between the two attitudes. "Lord, now help me. I want to be loving toward Ron, yet faithful to you and to myself. Guide me in this."

A commitment to Jesus Christ never means "happily ever after." In fact, Jesus promised we'd have troubles and problems. He also promised his presence. We can overcome—not once, but continually. Through Christ's help we become continually victorious.

One morning I walked past a Sunday school class of grade schoolers. They were singing a chorus I hadn't heard for years. But it still spoke the truth of life's possibilities: "With Christ in the vessel I can smile at the storm . . ."

We'll always have storms and problems. But like the disciples in the small boat, we have Jesus there to say, "Peace, be still." And hearing his command, "Peace," assures us that we—even people like me—can smile at the storms, because Jesus is with us.

Questions for Thought
and Discussion

1. "I'll never be the same again." Have you ever said those words? If so, how did you feel? How long did the sense of happily-ever-after last?
2. Why do you think people say, "I'll never be the same again"?
3. In the previous chapter, I asserted, "You can change." Now I say, "Yes, but..." Do you see a contradiction here? How can the two chapters be harmonized?
4. Can you share an example from your own experience of a time when great victory was won, yet there were recurring battles to maintain that victory?
5. I have shared the problem I have had over the years with temper. Do you think I'll ever be completely rid of my problem? Why?
6. Think of a problem area in your life. Read again the section called *"Preventive Measures."* Can you think of fortifications for yourself—made in advance? Can you think of other things I might have done in my situation?
7. Look at the section *"In the Situation."* I admitted to Gary I had been angry. Do you think I should have said, "Yes," when Gary asked, "I hurt your feelings, didn't I?"
8. Look at *"After-the-Fact-Measures."* Think of your own areas of weakness. What can you do, when you've failed in these areas, in order to help you succeed the next time?
9. Read the section on the game "Fantasy." Would you find this helpful in your particular problem?

23

Dreams Are Prayers
Your Heart Makes

"You become what you think about the most," the speaker said
in an offhand way as he went on to a major point. I've forgotten
the rest of his message, but those words stuck with me.

As I examine my own life and consider my reflective thoughts
(including my daydreams) and silent hopes, I realize they've
fairly well determined the direction of my life. Maybe it works
that way with all of us.

Once in a while someone dares to tell his dreams. I remember
the famous sermon Martin Luther King preached in Washing-
ton, D.C. in August 1963—bold words for that day!

> This afternoon I have a dream. It is a dream deeply rooted in the
> American dream. I have a dream that one day right down in
> Georgia and Mississippi and Alabama the sons of former slaves
> and the sons of former slave owners will be able to live together
> as brothers. . . . I have a dream this afternoon that the brother-
> hood of man will become a reality in this day.

This kind of dreaming became clear to me in the late 1960s
when I did graduate work at Atlanta University—an almost
exclusively black school. The few whites and orientals there
knew the feeling of being a minority group. But in the two
years I worked there on my degree I never felt pushed aside or
discriminated against.

I did find the black students surprisingly open and yet dedicated to a purpose. I did my work in the school of education, where many of my fellow-students were teachers in the Atlanta school system. They often talked about their own students. I recall one woman saying that the favorite song of her fourth grade was the haunting theme from *Man of LaMancha,* "The Impossible Dream." Even as young as they were, her pupils had already begun to grasp the vision of their teachers and leaders—reaching for unreachable stars, fighting unbeatable foes, and righting unrightable wrongs.

I learned a lot about black people during that period of time. Many had a dream of equality. Some obviously chose wrong methods to achieve their goal. Some only dreamed and went no further. But it made me feel good to be among people who had dreams, who didn't mind talking about them and working toward bringing those dreams into reality.

Years ago I read the autobiography of Agnes de Mille. She had always wanted to be a dancer, but she had short legs and a heavy body instead of a dancer's lithe, willowy frame. So she became a choreographer, and kept on dreaming and working toward her dream of being involved in the dance. With the choreography for the musical *Oklahoma,* she swept in a new concept of dancing—one in which physical movement advanced the story instead of simply being an interlude.

Agnes de Mille started with a dream. Then she put her energy into making that dream a reality. I sense that same kind of dreaming in the life of the Apostle Paul. He writes in his letters of straining forward, moving ahead, not looking back (see Phil. 3:14), always yearning to be the most completely yielded Christian possible. Another time he wrote, "Imitate me as I imitate Christ."

I think other great men of God must have had the same kind of dreams. What of Joseph languishing in prison? Or David as he spent nearly twenty years running away from King Saul? These men had their dreams and they held on to them.

And what about you? Do you have an ambition? An unfulfilled desire? Why not take it out of the inner recesses of your mind, brush it off, and dream about it?

For us as Christians, our dreams are another form of praying. And if we keep listening to those secret dreams and pressing on, we can achieve. We can make them come true!

For instance, I can't remember a time when I didn't want to go to college. But it seemed impossible. My dad, having lost everything during the depression years, didn't do much better during the war years because of bad health. When I finished high school, I knew my parents didn't have the money to help me go to college; I didn't even ask. In those days there were few scholarship programs available.

So within a month after graduation I found a job working for Civil Service. It paid well—at least for a first job. But one day I looked at my boss. He had worked there twenty-seven years, and all of that time in one department. That was not for me! So I joined the Navy in order to receive veteran's benefits and go to school. And eventually I graduated from college.

In the service I talked to several others who had a similar dream. They wanted to get out of the military, go to school, find a field of work that suited them. But so few of them actually pursued the educational opportunities. They stopped dreaming. For me, to stop dreaming means to stop living the fulness that life offers.

Of course, some dreams are just fantasies with no real chance for fulfillment. For instance, I have a deep appreciation of music. When I've heard voices like those of the late Mario Lanza or of more popular singers like Jerry Vale, I've envisioned myself standing before an audience—singing and receiving thunderous applause. But, while I appreciate music, I can't sing well. I know my dream of being a great singer is pure fantasy. That's not the kind of dreaming I'm referring to here!

Dreams can be realized. They can happen when we put ourselves into the position to make them happen. But dreams, like prayers, entail work. D. L. Moody used to say that the world has yet to see what one man, totally yielded to God, can do. And he determined to be that man. He thought about it, prayed about it, and lived a life that made him available for God's use.

Another man who lived a dream was Jacob. He loved Rachel

and worked seven years for her father as a dowry. Then, on the wedding night, he married (he thought) a veiled Rachel and found out it was her older sister Leah. When he discovered the deception, he angrily stomped over to the father-in-law and complained.

"But that's the custom in our country," Laban answered. "The younger daughter can't be married first. You'll have to serve another seven years for Rachel." And Jacob did. The Bible records, "They seemed to him but a few days because of the love he had for her" (Gen. 29:20).

A few months ago I read an article in a writer's magazine about famous authors. Many of them—from Hemingway to Fitzgerald—stumbled around and suffered through thousands of rejection slips before they made their first sales. Even then, they had many difficult times before they really hit it big.

Dreams that come true are not the one-time-in-my-life type of dream. They begin with an inner desire, perhaps so deep that you almost hesitate to tell anyone else about it. But you press on. You shape your life to encompass your dream. And that's the real secret. You allow your dreams to shape your life.

My friend Jay realized a startling fact nearly twelve years ago: he didn't really love people, at least, not in the way God intended him to love. He helped others when it was convenient and found excuses when it wasn't. He spoke of his love for Jesus Christ, but one day he felt convicted for the shallowness of his commitment.

"I prayed that day, 'Lord, make me as loving as I can be. I'm not asking for a lot of talents or to be a great person, but I am asking you to make me a lover of people.'"

Jay prayed for several days, and after a few weeks he realized he didn't feel any differently toward people than he had before. He was the same person in the same situation.

"Okay, God, then I'll do what *I* can about it." When people talked to him, Jay attempted to show more interest in them. He said yes to requests more frequently than he had before. Recently when Jay shared with me he said, "I don't know when it happened. Maybe it came about gradually. But I know now what it means to care about someone other than myself. And I haven't stopped praying. I keep asking God to make me exemplify his love in my dealings with other people."

What do you want to do with your life? What kind of dreams are still alive? What are you doing about them?

I'd suggest that you examine those dreams. *Are they within the realm of possibility?* Marty's thirty-four years old. He has more schemes, plans, programs, ideas, and innovative concepts than probably anyone else I know. But none of them are very realistic. He's never carried out even one of them.

And that's the second step: *if they're realistic, what can you do about making them a reality?* Here's where prayer really comes into focus. Commit that dream to Jesus Christ's scrutiny.

A missionary friend of mine did that. He wanted to start preaching in a new territory. After a full year of constant praying for that area, several ideas occurred to him. He wrote the strategy out carefully. Then he walked into the mission church. Kneeling at the altar, he prayed for several minutes, asking divine guidance. He laid the paper out on the altar. "God, this is the only way I know to show you and myself how serious I am about committing my future plans to you. Now I wait for your guidance."

As he continued quietly, a sense of peace came over him. He had an answer. God would make the dream come into reality. He himself would work to make it happen. Within three months he had established a flourishing work among a primitive tribe.

Don't be sidetracked from your dream. This easily happens to all of us. Pray those dreams—every day! Don't just wish it were so.

In the church corridor I've heard someone say something like this: "If only I could be more like Edna. She's so patient and understanding." That's a great desire. But I wonder if the person speaking ever does anything to become like Edna? Does she work toward being patient? Does she pray for understanding?

It's not enough to want to be something else or somebody else. We need to keep the vision before us.

As I think back on that speaker who said, "You become what you think about the most," I'd like to rephrase it a little. I think I'd like to say, "You become what you *pray* about the most."

How are you praying?

Questions for Thought
and Discussion

1. "You become what you think about the most," is the first sentence of this chapter. Why do you agree or disagree?
2. Can you agree with the author that our dreams and day-dreams are also prayers?
3. Sit quietly for three minutes, eyes closed. What kind of dreams do you have? Do they seem realistic? Have you ever done anything about making them more than dreams?
4. What can you say to someone who has dreamed/prayed over a long period of time and had no success? Do the examples of Agnes de Mille, Hemingway and Fitzgerald help in understanding?
5. Ask yourself, "What do I want to do with my life?" Have you fulfilled any of your dreams? Do you have one or two that you want to see fulfilled? What specific things can you do toward making your dreams come true?
6. Evaluate the statement, "You become what you pray about the most."
7. Why do I suggest you pray your dreams every day?
8. Think of the minority group in your general community. What kind of dreams do you think members of this group have? If you were part of that minority, what dreams would you have?